Stephen Brook 22.2.67
Trinity College, Cambridge

$H) = /1.75$

THE RISE OF URBAN AMERICA

American History

Editors

JOHN HIGHAM
Professor of History in the University of Michigan

and

CARL DEGLER
Professor of History at Vassar College

THE RISE
OF URBAN AMERICA

Constance McLaughlin Green

HUTCHINSON UNIVERSITY LIBRARY
LONDON

HUTCHINSON & CO *(Publishers)* LTD
178-202 Great Portland Street, London W1

London Melbourne Sydney
Auckland Bombay Toronto
Johannesburg New York

First published in Great Britain 1966

*This book has been set in Bembo, printed in Great Britain
on Smooth Wove paper by Anchor Press, and
bound by Wm. Brendon, both of Tiptree, Essex*

TO BETSY

CONTENTS

ACKNOWLEDGMENTS

My debt to Carl Bridenbaugh, authority on American urban life in the colonial period, is overwhelming, and only less so to the other authors whose works, listed in my brief bibliography, cover shorter periods of time. In addition, my grateful thanks go to Dr Irving B. Holley of Duke University, whose critical reading of much of the text has been invaluable, and to Joseph L. Intermaggio of Washington, D.C., whose knowledge of the current urban scene has added substance to the last chapter.

Washington, D.C.   C.McL.G.

I

THE FIRST CENTURY OF

AMERICAN URBAN LIFE

In the densely populated world of the mid-twentieth century, the ubiquity of big cities has become a matter of course. When English trading companies and royal patentees were planting their first settlements in North America in the seventeenth century, European cities were still relatively few. Even after the term 'city', once limited to the seat of a bishop, broadened to include populous communities under other forms of corporate government, only London and Bristol in all England contained more than 25,000 inhabitants; and, irrespective of numbers, before 1700 scarcely a half-dozen English provincial towns displayed distinctly urban qualities. Yet by the opening of the eighteenth century, along the Atlantic coast of the New World five seaports had sprung up that embodied the essential features of an urban society. These cities in the wilderness, small though they were, had developed a commercial vigour, an appreciation of the amenities, and a civic spirit shown in a readiness to subordinate the individual's convenience to the common weal that set them apart both from the rural countryside of tidewater and from the frontier to the west. By 1740, moreover, following six or seven decades that had brought few significant changes to British provincial cities, each of the five colonial seaports had expanded in population and attained an affluence and urbanity impressive to the most sophisticated European visitor. Expecting to see clusters of crude cabins set in small clearings in the forest where wild beasts and savages lurked, he was astonished to find handsome brick, stone, or frame houses lining streets as well drained and paved as those in most prosperous Old World cities, bookshops, markets, wharves, taverns, and, perhaps most amazing of all, widespread intellectual curiosity among the upper classes.

The forces that created in the course of little more than a century centres of an urban civilisation on a nearly empty continent derived from the expansion of world trade in the seventeenth century under English and Dutch leadership. The permanent settlements along the Atlantic seaboard of North America were established at a time when western Europe was beginning to throw off the shackles of a feudal economy; they took root in an era in which joint stock companies were replacing kings and merchant princes as the sponsors of large-scale overseas ventures and when the credit system of modern capitalism was supplanting medieval methods of financing. Indeed, without the corporate form of business organisation to supply continuity and the financial backing of numerous shareholders, it is hard to see how such precarious undertakings could have succeeded. The beneficiaries were the English nation as a whole and the families who, in risking the very real perils of the New World, gained livelihoods and, in some cases, fortunes. The fortunes, with few exceptions, sprang from commercial enterprises centring in the young colonial towns.

Of the five communities that spearheaded this urbanisation in the seventeenth-century colonies the northernmost was Boston on New England's 'stern and rockbound coast' in Massachusetts Bay; the southernmost was the newer, much smaller settlement of Charles Town a thousand miles down the Atlantic seaboard in South Carolina. The other three were located between those geographical extremes—Newport in the Providence Plantations of Rhode Island; New Amsterdam, renamed New York in 1664 after the English conquest of New Netherlands; and William Penn's Philadelphia, on the Delaware River at the mouth of the Schuylkill. The Dutch settlement on Manhattan was five years old when the Puritans of the Massachusetts Bay Company started building their town in 1630.

Dissidents from the religious views of the Bay colonists founded Newport on Narragansett Bay in 1639. Royal patentees established Charles Town in 1680 at the place where, according to a South Carolina chronicler, 'the Ashley and Cooper rivers joined to form the Atlantic ocean'. Penn laid out the Quaker 'City of Brotherly Love' two years later.

More than age differentiated those embryo cities from each other. Just as each early came to be the metropolis of its province and the direct link with European civilisation 3,000 miles and some three months' voyage to the east, so from the very beginning each had distinctive characteristics born of its geographic setting and the nature of its hinterland. Each port had a sheltered harbour well adapted to the use of ocean-going vessels; the broad Delaware at Philadelphia's site was virtually an arm of the sea reaching up from Delaware Bay; at Charles Town, where ships loading or unloading had to resort to lighters before wharves were built in the 1690s, anchorage was safe for the largest ocean-going craft of the day; New York and Newport stood on islands, and Boston was connected with the mainland only by a narrow neck washed by the tides at high water and during storms. Each town, furthermore, was immediately affected by the aims of its sponsors and financial backers in England or Holland, and, above all, by the ideals, educational background, and religious convictions of the first settlers. Those initial differences not only influenced the character of later immigration and contributed to divergences in institutional development but were in turn modified by the influx of newcomers, chiefly Englishmen, Scotch-Irish, and Africans brought in as slaves.

In most realms of activity, Boston early outstripped every colonial rival. She kept that lead for a century, despite the Indian wars that twice before 1680 threatened her with extinction. Population rose from the 300 to 400 of the 1630s to 16,000 by 1742. She achieved commercial stature in the face of an unkind nature. Compared with the fertility of the areas adjoining the more southern settlements, the barrenness of the New England hinterland put her at a disadvantage from the first. Even firewood, that necessary defence against the bitter cold of New England winters, had become scarce in the immediate vicinity of the Bay by the 1670s, and produce from nearby

farms was rarely more than enough to feed the tillers of the soil and
their town neighbours.

Yet Bostonians quickly learned to turn handicap to profit by
developing shipbuilding and a far-flung carrying trade. Cod,
mackerel, and haddock netted on the Newfoundland banks were a
staple of that trade and laid the foundations of many a Boston
fortune. Salted down and packed in hogsheads, the best of the catch
went to Catholic Europe; the poorer grades, shipped to the West
Indies, became a mainstay of the diet on which planters fed their
slaves. In time, when New Englanders raised some surplus cattle,
salt beef was similarly marketable in the islands. Return cargoes
usually consisted of sugar, molasses, rum, port and Madeira wines,
and other European luxuries. Molasses, served with corn bread or
used in such famous dishes as Boston baked beans and Indian
pudding, sweetened the fare of every New England working-man's
family, and throughout the seventeenth century rum was the
standard beverage in every tavern along Boston's waterfront and
inland. As the principal port of entry, Boston was also the distributing centre of merchandise for the entire region.

Although crown functionaries after the Restoration marked the
noblest pines of the New England forests for masts for the Royal
Navy, lumber, turpentine, and ships' rigging supplemented the
articles on which Boston's trade throve from 1660 onwards. In
winter ox-drawn sledges moved heavy loads of logs over the snow-
covered countryside to the seaport whence sawn boards went to
England, barrel and pipe staves to the West Indies, and carefully
selected beams and planks to the local shipyards. Shipbuilding early
became a major source of the town's prosperity, as her shipwrights
learned to turn out not only sturdy fishing smacks but also skilfully
rigged, capacious merchantmen that commanded good prices both
at home and abroad. Not infrequently a captain-owner sold his ship
as well as his cargo in a foreign or distant colonial port and made his
way home with his crew as mate and hands on some New England-
bound vessel. Very occasionally a shipmaster defied the English
Navigation Acts by carrying to or from Europe goods which the
law restricted to markets in the mother country, but ordinarily
trade within the empire satisfied him. Privateers out of Boston

profited, furthermore, during the wars with France, and for a century ships of Boston registry were to be seen in every sizeable port of the hemisphere.

After 1720 Salem, on Massachusetts' northern shore, and Newport, to the south, began to offer a serious challenge to Boston's supremacy over New England commerce, but her investment capital, accumulated over the years, kept her in first place. Farm boys drawn to the sea gravitated towards her Long Wharf and, when their sea-faring days were over, settled into jobs in the ships' chandler shops, the warehouses, or merchants' counting rooms along the waterfront. Multiplying numbers of artisans and retail shopkeepers added diversity without changing the focus of business activity. In tide-encircled Boston, ran the saying, all streets led down to the sea.

In shaping the character of the community even more important than the singleness of economic interests was the basic homogeneity of Boston's population. Springing from the common background of her early settlers, that homogeneity was only slightly diluted by the trickle of Ulstermen which began about 1717, and only superficially altered by the nearly 2,000 Negro servants imported before 1720. The imprint of her English Puritan founders endured. Among them were men educated at Cambridge or Oxford and several who possessed modest means; the rank and file were of relatively humble origin. Religious faith bound the group together. They believed that in setting up a Biblical commonwealth in the wilderness they were carrying out God's will. To avoid interference from the Crown, Archbishop Laud, or their fellow shareholders in London, the leaders of the Massachusetts Bay Company brought the company charter with them to the New World. By 1634 they had set up a theocracy controlled by the clergy and principal laymen of the colony's established Congregational Church. Before 1647 only 'freemen' had a voice in town meetings and in the election of representatives to the General Court. Boston, home of the chief men of the colony, dominated newer towns as they sprang up. A brief rebellion against the autocratic Puritan regime ended in 1637 with the expulsion of dissenting sects and left the orthodox in command during the years of civil war, Roundhead parliaments, and the Protectorate in Enlagnd. In that interval the constant danger of

Indian attack and the hardships of frontier life united the people of Massachusetts Bay and strengthened the hold of the theocracy.

When the Restoration brought royal agents to New England to investigate the colony's doings, they found a series of closely knit communities constituting, under Boston's leadership, a virtually independent state, issuing its own currency, ignoring royal customs regulations, providing for its own defence by means of obligatory militia service, conducting its courts under an admixture of Mosaic and English common law, and excluding from its body politic all religious nonconformers. After the English capture of New Netherlands in 1664, mounting pressures from the Crown led Massachusetts magistrates to modify some of their procedures, but the autonomy of 'Emanuel's Land' crumbled in the next twenty years and disappeared in 1691 upon the appointment of a royal governor and other Crown officials. Yet the Puritan spirit lived on, chastened and gradually mellowed but otherwise little changed by the presence of royal dignitaries, multiplying Anglicans, and members of sects formerly excluded from local privileges. The Puritan clergy, so far from losing caste, continued to exercise extraordinary political influence, particularly in Boston. Their exhortations to stand fast against any threat to the liberties of the King's free subjects in the colony prepared the way for the American Revolution.

The very fanaticism that drove Antinomians and Quakers from the colony in its early years and later brought witches to the gallows grew out of the feeling of obligation to protect the sheep within the Puritan fold from the ravening wolves of heresy and simultaneously to preserve order, the handmaiden of righteousness. Every subscriber to God's covenant must share the responsibility. The town meeting was the chosen instrument. There freemen annually elected three selectmen to carry out the town's mandates and lesser functionaries such as night watchmen to patrol the streets after dark, enforce the curfew, and warn of fires. When growth in population called for closer surveillance, a town constable served during the day, committing the occasional disturber of the peace to the town lockup until the magistrates could mete out punishment—a day in the stocks, a fine, a public whipping, or, in extreme cases, a branding or expulsion from the colony. Although rough characters collected here as in all seaports, town officers kept roistering, thievery, and violence to a minimum; whoring, impossible to suppress altogether, flourished less openly than in most expanding contemporary communities. Sanitation also came under town regulation. Early ordinances established quarantines for ships arriving from plague-ridden ports, forbade householders emptying their slops into the streets or dumping garbage along the highways and waterfront, and specified the depth to which privy vaults must be dug. When property owners began to lay underground drains from their dwellings, and a civic-minded few constructed underground mains in several streets, town officials required householders to obtain licences to connect with the sewer mains, lest faulty work create a public nuisance.

By town vote every family had to equip itself with leather buckets for firefighting, and adult males were expected to join the bucket brigade when an alarm sounded. After a disastrous conflagration in 1711, the town bought three new suction engines and, under the direction of ten fire wards, founded what was essentially a public fire department. On moonless nights lanterns at the thresholds of houses lighted the main thoroughfares. The town placed restrictions upon the width and weight of carts threading their way through the narrow streets and forbade shopkeepers to pile merchandise at their doorsteps where it might obstruct the public passage way, for the streets of the burgeoning seaport followed the narrow winding paths leading to the common where freeholders pastured their cows. If parsimony and official ineptness were sometimes evident in town administration, and if affluent men grumbled periodically over increases in their 'rates', still the self-respecting Bostonian recognised his duty and behaved accordingly. He might smuggle valuable goods into port under the noses of royal customs collectors, but he would not dream of evading local taxes and would serve conscientiously if elected to local office.

Overseers of the poor took charge of providing for the town's aged, crippled, or helpless indigents. In keeping with the general principles spelled out in the Elizabethan Poor Laws, only bona fide residents were entitled to public relief. Before 1700 the overseers usually paid a flat sum per head to householders willing and able to board and clothe the town's adult dependents and infants; later that plan gave way to placing them in a town poor house. Children over five or six years old were bound out to masters who contracted to see to their schooling as well as to their learning a trade or house-keeping skills. Although private charity often offered supplementary help and sometimes assisted non-resident paupers, a rigid watchful-ness over claims on the town purse marred the workings of the system. But outside New England no colonial town freely acknow-ledged public responsibility for its derelicts or, as a matter of course, tendered care to its needy at public expense.

Probably more lastingly important to her future was Boston's attitude towards schooling. Most of her first settlers could read the Scriptures, but unless their children also could turn to that infallible guide, how could a wonder-working Providence prevail in the New Jerusalem? An educated clergy was even more essential. So Harvard College came into being in 1636 to train young men for the ministry; for its support the General Court imposed upon every settlement in the colony an annual levy payable in Indian corn. At the same time some forty-five of Boston's richest inhabitants sub-scribed £40 to start a free school at which youths could prepare for college, and in 1643 freemen of the town voted to improve an island in the harbour for the maintenance of 'a free schoole'. Later adopted by most Massachusetts towns, the system thus inaugurated insured permanent income for public education by lease or sale of town lands. The passage of a school law in 1647 reinforced the scheme. Town monies in 1652 built a schoolhouse and a dwelling for the master of the institution known today as the Boston Latin School. There, under a succession of gifted masters, boys received an excep-tionally thorough secondary education. For years small children, on the other hand, learned the rudiments of reading and spelling at home or in a 'dame school', where a housewife taught her neigh-bours' children along with her own. But in response to repeated demands, in the 1680s the town opened two free schools for boys below the Latin School level. By 1690 Boston was spending half the town's 'standing charge' for public education. Because of the scarcity of hard money, a number of rate payers met their obliga-tions by boarding a teacher for a month or more, supplying firewood for the schoolhouse or undertaking repairs to the building.

Private schools which began to appear in the 1660s fortunately widened the opportunities for the daughters of well-to-do families, for Bostonians' dedication to education stopped short of extending it to females beyond the three Rs of dame school. Yet before 1720 the town was supporting five free schools with 600 pupils, and before 1739 *Instruction for Children, Or The Child's and Youth's Delight, Teaching an Easy Way to Spell and Read True English*, had gone through twenty-six editions. A school committee elected at town meetings appointed the dominies, saw to the upkeep of the buildings, purchased supplies, and watched over pupils' progress. While the system failed to reach all children and the human jetsam and flotsam washed into the port yearly added difficulties, literacy in seventeenth- and eighteenth-century Boston stood higher than anywhere else in the Western world.

As early as 1647 Boston had two bookshops, and by 1711 thirty-four more. Imports from London comprised much of the stock—school texts, Bibles, books on religious subjects, navigation, law, or medicine—but from the 1670s onwards local printers augmented the supply of sermons, pamphlets, almanacs, occasionally copies of *Pilgrim's Progress* or Anne Bradstreet's poems, and, in 1719, a reprint of *Tales from Mother Goose*. Books and pamphlets not immediately sold to customers at the Bay went out in pedlars' packs to the backcountry. While private libraries grew, the town made purchases for the Boston Public Library in the Town House where town meetings took place; when the building burned in 1711 public funds replaced the lost volumes and provided new accessions. 'Humanity and knowledge of letters', wrote an English visitor in 1719, 'flourish more here than in all other English plantations put together.' Well before then developments in experimental science were absorbing the attention of Boston intellectuals. The Reverend Cotton Mather corresponded with members of the Royal Society in London and, after discovering in one of its publications an account of smallpox inoculation, persuaded Boston physicians to adopt the new method. Meanwhile a group of younger Harvard graduates published in the *Philosophical Transactions* papers dealing competently with astronomy and natural history. Direct contacts by sea with Europe kept

Bostonians in close touch with the main intellectual currents of the age.

As mounting fortunes induced a measure of worldliness, Boston's upper classes indulged in fine clothing, handsome coaches, and beautiful and rare household furnishings. Wealthy merchants sat for their portraits, gave and attended elaborate balls, purchased clavichords and fiddles in order to enjoy evenings of music at home, stocked their cellars with vintage wines and their library shelves with the latest books from England, and accorded vast respect to learned men in the community. But if convictions about their own importance fostered disdain for the riff-raff crowding about the port, an enduring sense of duty, ingrained in the Puritan, impelled the well-born to help underlings to improve themselves.

The appearance of local newspapers offered the lower ranks of society one means of widening their horizons. The *Boston News Letter* issued its first number in 1704 and had no competitor until the *Boston Gazette* began publication in 1719 under the direction of the postmaster. Before mid-century out-of-date items reprinted from European papers filled most of both sheets, but local advertisements inserted by school teachers, dancing and music masters, and purveyors of other special services informed readers of the amenities available at home and thus fostered awareness of the varied opportunities open to ambitious men. Although issues rarely ran to more than 300 copies each, they were passed from hand to hand, read avidly in the taverns and coffeehouses, and sent on to people in other colonies. In time to come these news sheets would be major vehicles for spreading the doctrines of the Revolution throughout the American colonies. In the interim they strengthened Boston's position as a commercial and cultural centre of the New World.

Newport, founded in 1639 by victims of Massachusetts bigotry, grew in the course of a hundred years from a village of 96 souls to a town of 6,200, an increase so modest, measured solely by population, that she remained a pigmy compared with Boston. The Narragansett Bay settlement nevertheless gradually attained an influence in the colonial world out of all proportion to her size. Her mounting commercial power, her well-ordered community life, and the material and intellectual graces with which her leading families surrounded themselves combined to give her a significant place in early American urban history.

In this 'cage of unclean birds', as Governor Winthrop of Massachusetts characterised the Rhode Island settlements, religious toleration prevailed from the beginning. Newport's first families looked upon churches as essential to social discipline, but after initially organising as liberal Congregationalists, most of them joined the Society of Friends. At all periods they accepted in their midst 'Paedobaptists', Protestant splinter sects, a Jewish congregation of a half-dozen families who built a synagogue in the 1660s, and Anglicans who came somewhat later. If Boston derived benefits from an enforced religious unity, the freedom of thought and practice prevailing in this 'receptacle for people of severall Sorts and Opinions' endowed Newport with a true urbanity long before she was counting her inhabitants in more than hundreds. Her readiness to consider ideas on their merits made her the enemy of orthodox New England but attracted to her men of courage and vision. Her clergy combined spiritual and intellectual attributes of a very rare order. George Berkeley, famous Dean of Londonderry, stopping off in 1729 en route to a mission in the West Indies, was so charmed by his courteous reception and the genuinely religious atmosphere of the town that he prolonged his visit to three years. During that time his sermons drew eager listeners to the Anglican Trinity Church, while his learning widened townspeople's intellectual interests.

The education of children preoccupied Newport no less than it did Boston. In fact the younger town acted before the older in setting aside land for school support. In 1640 rentals from parts of a hundred-acre plot financed a first school for youths of 'the poorer sort'. Closed when its Oxford-trained master returned to England, it reopened in 1663. Thereafter, except for a few brief intervals, a schoolmaster, paid from the proceeds of sales or leases of the school land, taught elementary subjects to Newport children. Individual gifts and further town land grants after 1700 built a Latin School and another school which was less advanced. Denominational schools also appeared in the 1730s, but 'young gentlewomen' and sons of the well-to-do usually finished their education at one or another of the excellent boarding schools in Boston.

Like all New England settlements, Newport chose selectmen to carry out decisions reached in town meeting. Unlike towns under the rule of the Massachusetts theocracy, she acknowledged as participants in town government all newcomers who acquired property and settled permanently in the community. At every stage regulations were fewer or simpler than Boston's, chiefly because the smaller town saw no need for extensive official supervision. A single constable sufficed until King Philip's War in 1676 flooded the island with refugees fleeing from the marauding Indians on the mainland; the constabulary then doubled for a year or two, and after 1680 a watchman patrolled the streets at night. Despite the preponderance of frame buildings, they were set far enough apart to safeguard against fire; the appointment of 'viewers of Laders & chimneys' in the 1670s was a further precaution. After a serious fire in 1730 the town purchased the newest make of pumping engine, erected a building to house it, and established engine companies. When street paving began in the early years of the eighteenth century, an ordinance designed to preserve the costly surfacing stipulated a miminum width of six inches for cartwheels. Unhappily the neglect of drainage together with the depredations of scavenging swine and dogs running at large turned the thoroughfares into a noisome barnyard, more like those of congested old European cities than the streets of other villages in the New World.

In caring for the town's indigents, on the other hand, Newport had an outstanding record. Although her pauper families could be counted on a selectman's fingers in the seventeenth century, and later resolute refusal to permit persons likely to become public charges to settle in the town kept their number small, public provision was generous for legitimate residents in need of help—widows, orphaned children, and impoverished aged people. Church and individual benevolence eased their lot further. A fund raised by deducting sixpence monthly from the wages of Rhode Island seafarers, moreover, enabled the town to help sailors taken ill in port and left behind penniless when their ships sailed.

The paucity of paupers was but one of several signs of Newport's prosperity. Yet during her first half-century much of her commerce was confined to exchanging the foodstuffs grown in the neighbour-

hood for European goods imported into Boston. That economic
vassalage to Massachusetts Bay lessened only little by little as merchants began to extend their coast-wise trade southward to the
Carolinas and to ship to Barbados and Nevis surpluses of Rhode Island
beef, pork, dairy products, horses, lumber, and candles. When the
Anglo-French conflict widened at the end of the century, the protected anchorage in Narragansett Bay sprouted privateers, an ever-
increasing number of them built in local shipyards. In the wake of
profitable privateering ventures, equally profitable illicit trade with
Caribbean buccaneers developed along with the wholly illegal
importation of African slaves. By 1720 Newport sea captains had
become the principal slave-traders of the North American continent.
When their ships discharged their wretched human cargoes at ports
in the plantation country, auctioneers quickly disposed of each lot.
A specified share of the proceeds usually went to crew members, the
rest to captains and mates. So some Newporters amassed fortunes
and ordinary seamen with a modicum of luck and judgement might
turn a competence into something more substantial. Bibles usually
accompanied the mariners on their long voyages to and from the
African coast. The God-fearing at home as well as at sea looked
upon the trade as Christian, a means of bringing heathen to the
Gospel. While persons of substance in the town of the mid-eight-
eenth century generally used Negro rather than indentured white
servants, manumission left relatively few blacks as slaves.

From 1720 onwards local shipyards and locally owned merchantmen dominated the economic life of southern New England;
Rhode Island, remarked one observer, was Newport. Her thrifty
families put some of their accumulating wealth back into business
enterprises, but much of it went into building handsome mansions
filled with choice Old and New World furnishings. There, in a
setting of decorum and dignity, learning and the arts occupied men's
leisure. At the same time rich townsmen put up country houses in
the immediately outlying area, especially along the hook of land
that sheltered the harbour from winter gales but lay open to delight-
ful sea breezes during the hot months of the year. As news of that
attraction spread among Newporters' business associates in South
Carolina and Georgia, and Southern planters began in the 1730s

to summer at Narragansett, the town took on a polish and sophistication that would remain her hallmark for the next 175 years.

Manhattan's development followed a rather different course. In addition to a magnificent natural harbour, the island offered settlers two advantages denied the New England towns: fertile soil extending over a wide adjacent territory and easy access to the interior of the continent by way of the river named after its explorer, Hendrik Hudson. When the Dutch West India Company planted a depot at the tip of the island in 1607, company plans encompassed only a trading post where carefully regulated barter with the Indians would net the company profits from the exchange of knives, blankets, and gewgaws for beaver, otter, and other valuable furs. With that objective in mind, so far from encouraging the rise of a self-governing community surrounded by the comforts and amenities of European civilisation, company directors preferred to keep tight administrative control over the settlement and to limit expenditures for streets, sanitation, and similar services. The consequence was long-lasting; for 150 years appointed officials exercised arbitrary authority over the town. Company directors sent out from Holland took command until 1653, then a burgomaster and schepens selected by the West India Company from among New Amsterdam's thousand-odd inhabitants, and, after the surrender to the English in 1664, mayors and councilmen chosen by the royal governor of the Province; even after a new charter in 1731 widened the town bounds, vested in the town corporation a lucrative ferry monopoly, and ostensibly gave property owners a voice in local affairs, the royal governor succeeded in keeping in his own hands the appointments to the principal municipal offices. Autocratic rule, however, had little effect upon the town's growth.

Three hundred souls in 1630, some 2,400 in 1660, about 5,000 at the end of the century, and a total of 11,000 forty years later spelled a notable increase, and, despite some reverses, commercial activities generally kept pace with it. New Amsterdam had early brought Long Island and most of the Connecticut settlements along the Sound into her business orbit. Although the decline and eventual collapse of shipbuilding and the loss of the fur trade to the frontier outpost a hundred miles up the Hudson River at Albany checked

New York's economic expansion during the first decades of English rule, her commerce regained vitality early in the eighteenth century. By shipping through Boston, Knickerbocker merchants found markets for their 'flower and bisket' in the Southern colonies and the West Indies, and for furs and whale oil in European ports. Concerted efforts to shake off dependence on New England shippers met with considerable success after 1730 when New Yorkers began to import in English bottoms direct from London and Bristol and to dispatch return cargoes of flour and meat. Simultaneously retail shops multiplied, and gold- and silver-smiths, cabinet-makers, and boot, shoe, and harness makers proved themselves able to compete with importers for the patronage of rich residents.

New Netherlanders and the traders and adventurers who drifted in and out of the port were a more diverse lot than the Englishmen who settled New England. When New Amsterdam became New York, Manhattan rapidly took on a cosmopolitan air. It sprang from the mixing of Dutch and English customs, from official declarations of religious toleration, and not improbably from the attitudes of royal governors, mayors, and councilmen towards public pastimes. The Dutch origins of the community, it is true, were clearly in evidence, audible in the language spoken in wealthy merchants' homes and visible in the crow-stepped roofs and gables of the dwellings lining the narrow streets. But the heterogeneity of the population was equally evident, heightened after 1700 by several thousand Negro slaves, by English and Scotsmen released from military service in Europe after the Treaty of Utrecht, and by a stream of indentured servants pouring in from North Ireland and the Palatinate in the 1720s. Members of the Dutch Reformed Church long outnumbered those of other denominations, although Anglican hostility and political entanglements in the 1690s threatened for a time to invalidate the Toleration Act of the 1660s. New York nevertheless was a place of many faiths, not only Dutch Calvinist and Anglican, but Quaker, Baptist, Huguenot, Lutheran, Scottish Presbyterian, and, despite a flare-up of local prejudice, Jewish from the 1730s onwards. Sectarian feuding in fact was more common than devoutness, and, in many a visitor's opinion, lack of any religion was the most common of all. In such a setting where religious tradition imposed few restraints, public amusements were subject to relatively little restrictive supervision. People of widely differing backgrounds and tastes were free to pick and choose. In the process they nurtured an urban spirit of live and let live.

New York was far and away the gayest of the colonial towns. Royal governors were eager to live as they had at home in London and accordingly encouraged social affairs—dinners, an occasional formal ball, cockfights, hunting, coaching, skating, and garden parties. Early in the eighteenth century troupes of actors began to stage plays, and in 1732 a fully fledged theatre opened. About the same time the popularity of private musicals led to two or three public concerts. High-ranking officials in the governor's entourage and a few wealthy merchants were the chief beneficiaries of the social round, but lesser people could enjoy inexpensive outdoor sports, the bonfires and the accompanying barrels of beer and wine tapped to celebrate the King's or Queen's birthdays, and always the gossip, tippling, gambling, and fellowship at the taverns. An easygoing joviality permeated every social class.

Easygoingness, however, cut two ways. Sanitation was sketchy and the ordinances enacted before 1730 ill-enforced. Although prosperity was so widespread that in 1713 only seventeen names stood on the town's relief rolls, care of the needy was always casual. When the town built an almshouse in 1736, the parsimonious scheme of employing it also as a workhouse destroyed much of its utility. The swarm of homeless children, ragged, dirty, and hungry, who roamed the streets in the 1730s, according to the *New York Journal*, would shock 'a moralised heathen'. Publicly financed education scarcely existed at all. After the Dutch surrender to the English, the free school New Amsterdam had opened in the 1650s turned into a Dutch Reform Church parochial school, and classes taught in Dutch were of no benefit to English children. The half-hearted attempts of the next seventy years to re-establish a system of public education were largely abortive. A poor child, if lucky, might learn to read and write in a charity school; children of well-to-do families both in the town and the surrounding countryside generally attended denominational or other private schools. Unquestionably the prevalence of two languages handicapped civic-minded New Yorkers in their endeavour to sponsor public schooling, but local aristocrats, well aware that the great European cities accepted no responsibility for free education for the lower classes, paid the periodic proposals scant attention.

The wish to parallel the sophistications of European centres, on the other hand, led wealthy men, Dutch and English alike, to form clubs, dabble in literary pursuits, and take an interest in science and in painting. Dilettantes, however, set the tone, stressing sociability and politics. If the appearance of the *New York Gazette* provided new topics of discussion after 1725, not until Peter Zenger started the *New York Journal* in 1734 did citizens bestir themselves to look at the community as a whole. The famous libel suit brought against Zenger which ended with vindication of freedom of the press not only gave his paper wide prestige but strengthened the position of middle-class New Yorkers who were increasingly ready thereafter to contest exclusive privilege.

The fourth settlement of the five to achieve stature in the New World lay nearly 850 miles south of New York in a swampy subtropical region of South Carolina. Because the site first chosen proved fever-ridden, in 1680 agents of the royal patentees moved the handful of settlers to a spit of land between the mouths of the Ashley and Cooper rivers and laid out Charles Town. There, also, the climate and marshy terrain bred malaria, and the first arrivals were hard pressed by 'ye Want of Victuals', but the fertility of the tidewater area and the vast hinterland beyond promised ultimate rewards to the colony's proprietors. Those rewards took years to materialise. Two decades after her founding, the village had only 1,100 inhabitants and had 'not as yett produced any Commodities fitt for ye markett of Europe, butt a few Skins . . . and a little Cedar'. Still, thanks partly to a migration of planters from Barbados, by 1710 Charles Town's population had reached 3,000, the exchange of forest products for West Indian luxuries was making headway, and the discovery that tidewater plantations worked by slave labour were well adapted to rice culture enabled large landowners to develop a staple crop for export. War with the Indians of the back-country very nearly destroyed the town between 1715 and 1717, but with the restoration of an uneasy peace deerskin again became an important article of trade, second only to rice until British bounties on indigo made that crop also profitable.

From about 1720 till the outbreak of the Revolution, rice, indigo, and skins formed the backbone of Charles Town's expanding commerce. Her merchants shipped direct to English or southern European ports. Return cargoes of furniture, English woollens, linen, and hardware sold almost as soon as they landed on the 'Battery', the sea wall built along the harbour's edge. Trade with the West Indies also throve, some of it traffic in slaves who had already had a measure of docility instilled by the whips of overseers on Barbados and other island plantations. Slave-traders out of Newport brought in most of the blacks shipped straight out of Africa. Because Carolina planters concentrated upon growing rice, foodstuffs raised in the Northern colonies and transported by Northern carriers supplied other items for the tables of Charlestowners and their neighbours. The Carolina port thus depended for her bread upon imports, and for her labour force upon slaves. It was the rise of a staple economy, the reliance on slave labour, and townspeople's lack of any control over local administration that determined the character of her development in the eighteenth century.

Narrow though her economic basis was, no other colonial settlement grew so rapidly between 1720 and 1742. While Newport's population increased 63 per cent, Charles Town's nearly doubled; but as approximately half her 6,800 inhabitants of the 1740s were Negro slaves, freemen, and white indentured servants who in time could become participating members of the community were fewer than in the Rhode Island town. Approximately a thousand Charlestowners were the descendants of French Huguenots who had emigrated after the Edict of Nantes; several hundred Scotch-Irish came in the 1720s and 1730s; English families, including those who had removed from Barbados, constituted most of the rest. Religious nonconformity was only briefly a divisive element. Although the Carolina charter decreed toleration, the establishment of the Anglican church in 1704 inaugurated twenty years of controversy, resolved, however, in the 1720s largely by the decision of prominent dissenters to join Anglican St Philip's which provincial taxes supported and powerful colonial officials attended. Religion on the whole sat lightly on Charlestowners. The amenities loomed larger.

Here was an aristocratic society. Although Negroes made up a third of New York's population in the 1720s, a sixth of Boston's, and a somewhat smaller proportion of Newport's, in the Northern towns the social structure rested not upon slave labour but upon a solid middle class. In Charles Town, on the contrary, where servile blacks formed close to a numerical majority, white artisans, craftsmen, and small shopkeepers were caught between the upper and nether millstone of the aristocracy and the slave population. Lacking substantial economic resources, they could not share the privileges of the former, and their position was steadily undercut from below by the increasing skills of trained slaves. Still all white men, however lowly their station, frequented the taverns, bet at cockfights, and, now and again, enjoyed the chance to see an exhibition such as an 'Ourangnogang (or Man of the Woods) tho' this . . . [was] a female of that species'. More sophisticated expensive pleasures were confined to the well-to-do.

After the building of a race track in 1735, young bloods organised a Jockey Club and competed for £100 purses or silver tankards. Later, Charlestowners laid out the first golf links in the colonies. By the mid-1730s two theatres were staging plays popular in London —*The Recruiting Officer, The Fair Penitent, Cato,* and others. Native talent performed at subscription concerts, and afterwards the gentry adjourned to elaborate balls; St. Cecilia's concert and ball in November yearly opened the social season. Portrait painters and landscapists able to produce decorative chimney pieces found generous patrons among rich Charlestowners as eager as their Northern counterparts to impress posterity and to embellish their houses. Yet before midcentury their dwellings, built of frame in a style imported from Barbados, were generally unpretentious. 'Galleries', that is, shallow balconies, ran the length of houses built one room deep with long windows and high ceilings in fashion to catch the sea breezes at all times. Placed with the narrow end to the street, the typical house of the wealthy resident stretched through a garden walled off from the highway and planted with fragrant semi-tropical flowers and shrubs; the kitchens, outhouses, and slave quarters stood apart at the rear of the lot. Within the drawing rooms conversation might range from the merits of a particular Madeira to provincial politics or, more rarely, to the recent findings of science. For, while multiplying bookshops nurtured urbanity, belles lettres had greater appeal than learning, and enjoyment mattered more than creativity. Carolina bred few writers. Literacy itself was somewhat of a luxury in a community where education was an upper-class prerogative. Two newspapers nevertheless began publication in 1732, and the owner of the *South Carolina Gazette* printed whole numbers of the *Spectator* and frequent selections from Pope, Swift, and John Gay.

A tax-supported school system was one of several public services considered essential in New England but denied to Charles Town. Inasmuch as the South Carolina charter made no provision for town government, the colonial Assembly passed upon every local measure, from the layout of streets to the enactment of a black code restricting slave activities. Charles Town, with over a quarter of all the inhabitants of the province, was represented by only four of the thirty members of the Assembly; her needs consequently netted little consideration from the majority of the planters and merchants who composed the legislature. For a generation they dismissed education as a family or church matter, and although in 1696 they voted £10 annually to support a school wherever commissioners deemed one needed, none appeared until 1712 when the 'Free School in Charles Town' opened. The name was misleading; the school masters offered pupils a sound classical education, just as the newly opened St Philip's Parish School gave children good training in elementary subjects, but both institutions charged for tuition. The Society for the Propagation of the Gospel paid the fees of most of the poor boys who attended either. In 1740 a former dancing master, moved by the exhortations of the great Methodist preacher George Whitefield, risked prosecution for violating the black code by undertaking to teach fifty-three Negroes to read; the courts allowed him to continue his self-imposed task, but apparently he abandoned it after a year or two. Thus charity, not public money, underwrote such schooling as the 'lower orders' in eighteenth-century South Carolina could hope for.

Sanitary regulation, fire protection, and poor relief also suffered under a system that allowed townspeople no control of local affairs. Charlestowners attributed the prevalence of illness to the 'nasty Keeping of the Streets', but the village was thirty years old before the provincial Assembly empowered the clerk of the town market to impose fines upon householders who let filth accumulate in the streets at their doors, and not until 1735 did an act sanction the construction of a sewer on Broad Street for which abutting property owners were to pay. A series of catastrophic fires near the turn of the century inspired the legislature to levy a tax on the town for the purchase of buckets, 'lathers', and a London-built engine, but only after a holocaust wiped out three-quarters of the provincial metropolis in 1740 did law require stone or brick for all new construction and the gradual replacement of all surviving frame buildings. Public provision for paupers was only less tardy. Just as the Assembly left the education of poor boys to charitable foundations, so the legislature looked to almsgivers to care for the poor until an act of 1712 levied a yearly tax on Charlestowners which the Vestry of St Philip's was to administer. Still the pauper population rose alarmingly during the next half decade, partly because three years of war with the Indians deluged the town with refugees from the surrounding countryside. In 1735 the Assembly, at last recognising her problem, voted provincial funds to build a 'Workhouse and Hospital'. The Vestry ran it efficiently and humanely, but in the 1740s poor relief cost the town nearly £1,800 yearly.

Whether Charlestowners would have managed better had they had freedom to act may be debatable. As matters stood, their impotence fostered civic irresponsibility. Public services operated largely for the benefit of the aristocratic few. The 'poorer sort', affected by the blight of slave competition, in the opinion of Eliza Pinckney were 'the most indolent people in the world, or they could never have been wretched in so plentiful a country'. Only plantation owners and exporters reaped its bounties. And by the 1740s the ambition of the merchant who had made a fortune in trade was to become a landed proprietor with a country estate in Charles Town's environs. As rice grown and harvested by slave gangs under the watchful eyes of white overseers was the money-making staple of the province, the planter held the key to the good life—leisure, a house in the outlying area, and handsome London-built coaches to take him and his family to and fro. Seat of the provincial government, and, as the one good port in the colony, the link with the Old World, Charles Town with her urban aura was and would remain the heart and centre of agrarian South Carolina.

Remarkable as was the growth of other colonial towns, Philadelphia's rise was the most spectacular. The latest launched, she achieved in sixty years a commercial and cultural eminence second only to Boston's and in seventy-five years became not only the foremost city in British North America but the second largest in the English-speaking world. The very lateness of her founding was an asset of sorts, for when William Penn, acting upon the privileges granted him by royal charter, engaged a surveyor to lay out the City of Brotherly Love, the wilderness and its perils had receded. Swedes, Hollanders, and Englishmen had already built scattered homes along the broad Delaware, and the Indians of the region had accepted them. Furthermore, among the first comers to Philadelphia were several wealthy men ready to put up wharves at their own expense and contribute to other improvements. And Penn's proclamation of religious toleration, coming from the Quaker proprietor, promised all sects an enduring sanctuary from persecution. Finally the rich earth of the hinterland stretching north, west, and south through well-watered valleys would soon earn for the region the title 'bread colony'. Thus fewer hazards lay in Philadelphia's way than was the case in the older towns.

Her development nevertheless was a source of wonder to witnesses of the transformation: the village laid out in 1682 on the wooded stretches of the upper Delaware a hundred miles from the sea had turned into a charming city of well-proportioned fieldstone, brick, or simple frame houses, handsome public buildings, and busy wharves where ships discharged goods and emigrants from Europe year after year and took on cargoes of Pennsylvania grain and beef, a city that combined vitality and elegance. And to a degree virtually unique in the eighteenth century, the cultivation usually confined to the upper levels of society permeated the strata below.

By the time Philadelphia was six years old she had nearly 4,000 inhabitants; by 1720 the number had risen to 10,000, and by 1742 to 13,000. Peopled at first chiefly by devout English Quakers, the town's rapid growth swiftly produced a diversity of religions, national origins, and economic status: Irish Quakers, Anglicans, Presbyterians, Baptists, Lutherans, a few Roman Catholics, and a flood of people without any religious leaning, Ulster Scots, Palatinate Germans, Negro slaves, indentured servants from northern Europe or Britain, impecunious artisans, and men of considerable means. Amidst the resulting ferment, religion played a steadily diminishing role until George Whitefield's arrival in 1739. While his sermons preached to audiences of as many as 10,000 townspeople and farmers from the surrounding countryside gave more force to the Great Awakening in and about Philadelphia than anywhere else in the colonies, the asceticism he advocated had very little long-term effect upon Philadelphians' preoccupation with worldly affairs. Just as early Quaker emphasis upon godliness and simple living failed to check a growing indulgence in luxury or to deter Quaker merchants from engaging in piratical commercial ventures during the Anglo-French colonial wars, so the counting house continued to have wider influence than the meeting house or any of the churches. Roads built into the back-country enabled shrewd Philadelphians to market the foodstuffs raised on farms eighty-odd miles inland and, in the fifteen years between 1727 and 1742, to expand shipbuilding on the Delaware from a total of 7 to 380 vessels, some of them of 200 ton burthen. Small wonder that Boston, lacking an equally productive hinterland, fell behind the younger town in the 1750s.

Craftsmen from abroad and from other colonial centres gravitated towards the Pennsylvania metropolis. Benjamin Franklin was not alone in choosing to move from Massachusetts Bay to the Delaware when he had acquired enough experience in his brother's print shop to strike out on his own. Neither Boston nor Philadelphia wanted for skilled artisans. Although obstacles to rising to eminence were greater in the eighteenth- than in the less complex seventeenth-century communities, Franklin's career illustrates the success a gifted young man might achieve without financial or social backing. The author of *Poor Richard's Almanack* observed that the Philadelphia gentry never accepted him as one of themselves, but he lived comfortably while he was still a little-known printer, and, as his writings and scientific experiments gradually brought him into the public eye, he attained a position of influence which his self-styled betters doubtless envied. His special talents quickly set him above his fellow artisans, but all the moderately competent had chances to better themselves. As in all the colonial towns, however, class distinctions were sharper in mid-century than earlier, and grumblings born of envy or of resentment at the treatment wealthy householders often accorded working men grew louder with every passing decade. Nor were fortunes accumulating in some hands but eluding others the sole source of dissatisfaction. The arrogant behaviour of royal officials angered the lower classes of the provincial capital. If it irked affluent Philadelphians also at times, more often they merely aped it.

Yet common people fared better in William Penn's city than in New York or Charles Town. From the standpoint of municipal authority or its exercise, to be sure, Philadelphia was as handicapped as Manhattan, and indeed her charter was modelled on New York's: a corporation of mayor and council responsible only to itself and with very limited taxing powers. So far as ordinances governing sanitation, drainage, street extension, and police and fire protection tell the story, the record of both town corporations was a chronicle of neglect, showing little more concern for the general public than obtained in Charles Town. As Philadelphia officials habitually acted belatedly, if at all, it was the concerted efforts of private citizens that created an orderly community where cleanliness, safeguards against fire and theft, care of the helpless, and free schooling for children were the rule. Although the Quaker 'spirituality' that impressed visitors in the 1690s faded as secularism spread, the Quaker sense of far-reaching community responsibility endured long after the Society of Friends ceased to dominate the town.

While Quaker business acumen was a major factor in developing her economic prowess, Quaker humanitarianism left an equally strong mark upon Philadelphia. During her early years, Friends provided homes for the indigent in private families. When that system became impractical because of the swelling tide of immigrant paupers, the Philadelphia Meeting built an almshouse and enlarged relief for needy people not requiring institutional care. Twice over, the Pennsylvania Assembly authorised public expenditures for poor relief, and twice over the mayor and council concluded that Quaker generosity was furnishing everything necessary. In 1732, however, abetted by a loan from the Assembly, city officials erected a public almshouse and an infirmary with separate quarters for the insane; and several years later when a provincial act broadened municipal powers, the corporation fixed poor rates at a figure high enough to enable conscientious Overseers of the Poor to make the almshouse a model.

Within a decade of Philadelphia's founding, the Quaker Meeting also developed a system of sound elementary and vocational education. The William Penn Charter School when opened in 1701 admitted 'all children and servants, male and female, whose parents, guardians and masters, be willing to subject them to the rules and orders . . . the rich [to be instructed] at reasonable rates, and the poor to be maintained and schooled for nothing'. Voluntary subscriptions and Quaker legacies supplied ample funds. Classes covered not only elementary subjects but 'good literature . . . languages, arts & Sciences'. Without establishing a tax-supported system, Philadelphians sponsored a dozen other excellent schools to which scholarships were numerous; Penn Charter and at least two other church and non-sectarian institutions admitted Negro pupils. And the private schools for girls were the best in the colonies.

In so literate a community bookshops flourished, and private libraries grew. After Quaker influence declined, the classics, belles lettres, history, and scientific treatises competed successfully with religious works for space on Philadelphians' shelves. In 1719 the *American Weekly Mercury*, the third newspaper to appear in the colonies, added current reading matter; in the 1730s the city had two more, the short-lived *Philadelphische Zeitung*, and the *Pennsylvania Gazette* which Benjamin Franklin turned into a lively and influential organ. While men of the wealth and learning of James Logan and John Bartram, creator of the first botanical garden in the colonies, contributed scientific articles to the *Philosophical Transactions*, Franklin, highly conscious of the talents to be found among poorer

B

men, organised a group of witty, literary-minded artisans and
tradesmen into the Leather Apron Club, or Junto, to discuss philosophy, politics, and poetry. The interchange of books among the
Junto inspired the founding of the Library Company, subscriptions
to which enabled its officers to purchase and loan to members books
otherwise practically unobtainable in North America. Although
Quaker objections kept the theatre from taking root as it had in
Charles Town and New York, after 1730 harpsichord and violin
concerts in private houses supplemented the public performances
German and Swedish musicians had given occasionally for a number
of years.

As wealth accompanied by taste increased, the patronage of
painters spread rapidly, and when the Pennsylvania Assembly in
1730 appropriated money to build a State House, Gustavus Hesselius,
the most noted artist in the colonies of his day, received a commission to decorate the interior with carvings and paintings. Thanks
to the talent and skills of master builders and accomplished gentle-
men amateurs, several public buildings attained an architectural
distinction unmatched elsewhere in the New World and rare in
England itself. Philadelphians succeeded in adapting the chaste
classicism of Palladio and Vitruvius to designs that took convenience
into account without marring the pleasing balance upon which
English Georgian architecture put special stress. In physical appearance Philadelphia in mid-century was at once the most substantial-
looking and beautiful city on the continent.

Each of the five leading towns of the colonies thus developed
characteristics distinctly her own—in architecture and overall
appearance, in intellectual interests and emphasis upon some of the
amenities at the expense of others, in religious and social attitudes,
in forms of municipal government, and, to a lesser extent, in
economic organisation. But differences were fewer and less basic
than similarities. True, the plantation system in the Deep South gave
Charles Town a somewhat different commercial focus from that of
the Northern communities; true also, Boston before 1715 occupied
a unique position as middleman for all the English settlements on the
mainland. Nevertheless the urban spirit emerging in the principal
towns created common points of view and minimised divergences.

No matter what the location or the founders' immediate aims, the life-blood of each was commerce. That in itself forged a bond among them. In the 1740s, from the recently founded colony of Georgia below South Carolina to the New Hampshire settlements of northern New England, newer towns were beginning to compete with the early leaders; Augusta, Georgia, at the head of navigation of the Savannah River, was intercepting some of Charles Town's trade with the hinterland; Norfolk in Virginia and Annapolis, Maryland, on Chesapeake Bay were expanding as outlets for tobacco and foodstuffs—in Annapolis's case reducing the control Philadelphia exercised over the commerce of the bread colonies; Salem and Portsmouth were obliterating Boston's monopoly over northern New England's commerce; and the rising power of Providence at the head of Narragansett Bay was shrinking Newport's status by cutting her off from direct contacts with the farming settlements in the interior. Yet the five provincial centres of the seventeenth-century colonies set the pattern for the rest.

With the exception of Newport, each of the older seaports still served in mid-century as the main channel of communication between the Old World and the remote frontier settlements, even while the peopling of the hinterland was interposing an ever-broadening band of farming country between the seaboard and the clearings in the wilderness on the frontier itself. But whereas settlers of rural and frontier areas generally turned their eyes westward towards the virgin lands awaiting occupancy, the city dwellers looked eastward towards overseas markets and the sources of supplies available to the New World only through importation. This contrast in outlook set the young colonial cities apart from the agrarian and sparsely settled back-country and strengthened their ties to each other. Indeed the major provincial capitals not only resembed one another in their modes of life but long had a closer affinity to Europe than to the frontier, for the Atlantic Ocean was a lesser barrier to the movement of people, goods, and ideas than were the vast westward-stretching forests of the continent. Tidewater Virginians, it is true, shared many of the tastes and intellectual interests of townspeople. The landed gentry whose plantations bordered on inlets and rivers shipped their tobacco direct to England from their own wharves and received in return modish London clothes, fine household furnishings, books, and news from the European urban world. As the Virginia gentleman at many times of the year had more leisure than his town counterparts, he had more time to read, converse, and correspond with learned friends. His was an urbane, semi-urban atmosphere in a rural setting. Moreover, at court sessions in Williamsburg, capital of the Old Dominion, planters rubbed elbows with country lawyers and piedmont farmers and so widened the reach of their ideas. As communication between seaboard and the interior became easier during the 1730s and 1740s, a continental unity began to emerge.

Despite differences in the views of the equalitarian back-country and the class-conscious towns, the seaports, though containing only 5 per cent of the colonial population in 1742, remained the unifying centres of colonial life. By comparison with European cities, their social order was flexible. A woman born in poverty need not be a Moll Flanders to reach an unassailable social position; more than a few tradesmen's daughters married into the gentry, and well-dowered heiresses occasionally married their fathers' clerks without permanent loss of caste. While greed, envy, sloth, and vice were ever present, the intellectual challenge in the towns more than offset their seaminess. Perhaps because chances to obtain an education were relatively easy, a respect for learning permeated all ranks of town society. Contacts with persons of varied experience widened mental horizons in a fashion impossible for farmers and frontiersmen engaged in an unremitting struggle with primitive nature. Crudity and violence marched hand in hand with refinement and self-imposed discipline in the urban centres, but an all-pervasive vitality was their most noticeable quality. If their intellectual activities and attainments in literature and the arts were meagre in comparison with the London of the Augustan Age, they were still far richer than those to be found in most English provincial cities.

Britons who had never set foot in America rarely if ever comprehended the dimensions of this achievement. Most of them apparently thought America still little more than wilderness, important primarily as a source of raw materials. Colonial townsmen might readily acknowledge that the boundless resources of the New World had

created their opportunity, but they knew also that courage, imagination, and hard work had been essential to putting it to use. They
assumed that all Englishmen recognised them as at least equals and
shared their pride in the extraordinarily swift rise of an overseas
urban civilisation.

2

FROM COLONIAL ENTREPÔTS TO
CITIES OF A NEW NATION

The changes in the thinking of western Europe which sparked the planting of colonies in North America ignited a powder train that exploded in a revolution during the second half of the eighteenth century. In the words of an eminent American historian, 'the revolt against monarchy, aristocracy, and authority that we call modern times' reached far beyond the American continent and had repercussions in every segment of Atlantic civilisation. To this revolt no one group contributed more than the young cities of the rebelling thirteen British colonies. Over a span of years they and the Virginia planters together organised the resistance that burst into war with 'the shot that was heard round the world'. And when peace came, the rebuilding of a stable society in an insecure new nation fell largely to leaders in the towns and Virginia statesmen.

The social revolution that gave birth to a new republic was germinating in the late 1740s, but the struggle between France and Britain for control of a continent submerged open conflict between mother country and colonies and partly concealed the growing cleavages within the colonial world between town and country and class and class. In the twenty years preceding the final victory over France in 1763, intermittent war subjected virtually all British colonials to recurrent danger and some economic tribulation. Service with the colonial militia and naval expeditions sent out from the seaports cost lives; marauding Indian tribes allied with New France harassed thinly populated frontier towns; French privateers harried American shipping and checked the flow of imports necessary to the well-being of townsmen and farmers alike. Penniless cripples, widows, and orphans swarmed in the towns where, despite theoretical bars against transient paupers, they could count on receiving protection and charity. Boston felt obliged to provide for refugees from Nova Scotia, Charles Town for homesteaders fleeing from Cherokee tomahawks, and all the seaports had somehow to accommodate growing numbers of disabled seamen. Yet during the 1740s and 1750s homesteaders steadily pushed farther westward, secondary towns multiplied, and the overall population of the five major cities grew from the 53,380 souls of 1743 to 72,880 in 1760, a numerical increase far greater than that in English cities. For the American ports were still the essential links between Old World and New and the chief distributors of goods to the interior of the continent. And while war stripped some men of fortunes, it made money for others.

For the seaport towns privateering was one wartime source of wealth. When a captain returned to Newport from the Caribbean in 1743 with news of a prize that had netted every sailor on his schooner 500 pieces of gold, other Rhode Island shipmasters and merchants hastened to obtain letters of marque and reprisal. A year or two later a sloop sent out by two Bostonians brought back a prize of 471,000 milled dollars contained in 163 sea-chests. Although Philadelphia Quakers disliked private warfare, Anglicans and Presbyterians in the City of Brotherly Love invested in several privateering voyages that produced rich booty, in one case loot valued at £135,000 sterling. South Carolina commissioned very few privateers, but Charles Town shipyards prospered by refitting Northerners' vessels that put in for repairs. Of all the ports New York sought prizes on the high seas most enthusiastically and longest; in 1759 alone, 48 privateers manned by 5,760 seamen put out from Manhattan. Elsewhere merchants gradually abandoned the enterprise when competition began to reduce its rewards, losses by capture increased, and other ventures, notably smuggling, promised more certain profit.

Trade with the enemy was the principal form of smuggling. The Crown labelled it treason, but a good many Americans saw nothing reprehensible in continuing to sell provisions to the French West Indies or Cape Breton or New Orleans. By landing their return cargoes surreptitiously, shipmasters avoided customs duties and ship owners could undersell competitors who imported sugar, molasses, and rum through legal channels. A flag of truce, purchasable from venal royal officials in Philadelphia, New York, and other places, generally insured the illicit trader against interference from the Royal Navy, as the flag indicated that the ship was transporting prisoners of war for exchange. In the 1740s Newporters were the most successful practitioners of the smuggler's skills; as one merchant confided to an agent in 1748, with a truce flag on the ship's mast a single voyage 'If I effect a Cargo of Sugars will clear upwards of Twenty thousand pounds'. Bostonians in turn managed to pursue considerable illicit commerce chiefly with Cape Breton and the French sugar islands, but during the 1750s New Yorkers and Philadelphians took the lead, inasmuch as royal officials there not only winked at the trade but frequently held shares in the ships carrying it on.

Government contracts for Army and Navy supplies also paid well. Merchants in political favour grew rich from furnishing food, clothing, shoes, and other equipment to British troops stationed in Boston and Albany. When New York became the 'general magazine of Arms and Military Stores' and principal headquarters of the Redcoats, Gothamites with proper family connections amassed fortunes without running risks, 'the military', observed a customs official, 'being exceedingly public spirited in the consumption of strong liquors'. In fact, New York's rise to first place among American cities had its beginning in these years. She lost fewer ships than Newport or Boston and, unlike the Massachusetts town, suffered relatively little from mounting military expeditions paid for out of the provincial purse.

While shipbuilding expanded in some of the ports, manufacturing also attracted mercantile capital, as that form of investment appeared safer than seafaring ventures in an era of 'deranged trade'. Boston's and Salem's shipyards had been a mainstay of Massachusetts's economy for nearly a century, but Newport pre-empted much of their business in the 1740s and with it the auxiliary enterprises of rope-walks, anchor forges, sail lofts, and cooperage. Although the consensus was that Rhode Island ships were the soundest built, Philadelphia yards turned out scores of large vessels in the 1750s to replace those sunk or captured by the enemy. Charlestowners produced some small craft for inland river trade, and three or four New York firms built a few sea-going vessels, but neither town specialised in the industry, an omission which partly explains their backwardness in the arts and crafts. For the smithies and the woodworking shops that in time produced beautiful samples of the cabinetmakers' art, as well as cheap furniture to sell in the Southern colonies, were originally ancillary to shipbuilding. Rum-distilling, beer-brewing, and the manufacture of spermaceti candles from the head matter of sperm whales, on the other hand, had less direct connection with shipfittings, and all three were important industries of the mid-eighteenth-century colonies. Food processing, in turn, made headway, especially in Philadelphia. Flour, the barrels in which to ship it, and leather goods, a sequel to the butchering and salting of beef cattle for export, were the chief products, but along the upper Delaware and its tributaries iron furnaces, woollen-stocking-making shops, and several paper mills added to the variety of wares Philadelphia merchants marketed. Within the city several linseed oil mills and foundries making nails, axes, and other hardware also flourished.

Retail shops to meet the needs of the swelling population of the towns, and pedlars to carry goods into the back-country, multiplied as rapidly as did the articles for sale. Women ran a number of the shops. Sometimes wives of sea captains disposed of the yard goods, pins, thread, buttons, and shoes their husbands brought into port. Widows and spinsters managed shops selling millinery, tobacco, groceries, and garden seeds. In all the colonial centres this form of activity was one of the few ways in which a respectable woman could earn her living. Laying out the dead for the furniture makers who built the coffins was another occupation open to women, albeit one generally acceptable only to those of 'the poorer sort'. The pedlars, whether carrying their packs on their backs or riding pack horses with heavily laden saddlebags, were a source of irritation to city retailers who believed they prevented country people from coming into town to make purchases, but these travelling salesmen performed a valuable service, if only in keeping homesteaders in remote areas aware of developments on the seaboard. While a popular story told of a chapman who exchanged a gaudy piece of calico for a 'Banquet of Love' from a farmer's wife, barter was less common than in the seventeenth century.

Hard money was still scarce, but paper currency authorised in most of the colonies relieved the shortage somewhat, and scrip issued by 'land banks' eased it further. For colonial assemblies, in seeking means of paying troops for their services during the French and Indian War, hit upon a scheme of issuing the men certificates of title to acreage in Western lands. That the land was still in the hands of Indian tribes rarely troubled the beneficiaries. Scrip was the ordinary medium of exchange in the towns until Parliament forbade further issues of paper currency in the New England colonies and in 1764 declared all colonial paper money no longer legal tender. The act was a blow to the towns' commercial interests. Lacking sterling or perhaps Spanish pieces of eight acquired in the West Indian trade, a Bostonian, say, or a Philadelphian was hard put to it to meet his obligations to firms in distant places. Fortunately, among merchants engaged in large-scale transactions and with well-established connections, bookkeeping transfers of credit reduced the amount of cash that actually changed hands.

Despite economic uncertainties, the towns grew at a rate that encouraged constant building and rebuilding. The worst fire in colonial history wiped out the centre of Boston in 1760; a quarter of the town's dwellings and warehouses burned to the ground. Rebuilding, conducted under careful supervision to prevent repetition of the disaster, gave the Bay town a new look. Because spacious lots within the town limits were few, some of the new tenements, however, like the older, housed more than one family. Fortunately, three recently built public edifices escaped destruction—the handsome hall given to the town by the Huguenot merchant, Peter

Faneuil; Kings' Chapel, designed by Peter Harrison of Newport, which lost impressiveness only because the parishioners could not afford to crown it with the majestic spire its Georgian architecture required; and the 'Concert Hall' with an elaborately ornamented interior 'in the Corinthian style'. Charles Town also had to undertake extensive rebuilding following up the fire of 1740 and again after a destructive hurricane twelve years later. There, too, building regulations attempted to forestall further losses, although enforcement was not wholly successful. Most of the private dwellings that went up adhered to the Barbadian galleried style, but a number were far more spacious and elegant than those they replaced. The erection of St Michael's after St Philip's parish was divided in 1753 and the construction of an imposing State House added two beautiful public buildings. The town thus took on the visible dignity and the distinctive charm thereafter associated with the architecture of planter society.

In the seventeen years before 1760, New York more than doubled the number of her houses, partly in order to accommodate the British troops stationed at Manhattan. Called by several visitors 'the pleasantest and best built city in all British America', she presented an agreeable compactness. As rentals of urban property were highly profitable, the city corporation and private owners leased considerable stretches of land upon which builders erected rows of solidly constructed five- and six-storey brick dwellings. 'New houses,' an observer remarked, 'have been built in a more modern taste and many of the Gable-ends of the old houses, just as is done in Holland, have been new fronted in the Italian stile.' Her public buildings erected in the 1750s were the city's special pride. In the fields on Broadway beyond the Hudson 'Pallisadoes' a three-storey brick jail went up not far from new barracks big enough to house a regiment. A gambrel-roofed brick merchants' exchange topped by a cupola rose at the foot of Broad Street in 1752. Its architect, Robert Crommelin, also designed St George's Chapel with a 175-foot steeple and in 1756 began work on King's College, the first unit of the Columbia University of the future. Magnificently located near the banks of the Hudson, the college was able to admit faculty and students to the handsome Georgian building in the spring of 1760.

Philadelphia had already won a reputation for the quality of her architecture. The beautifully proportioned State House, finished in 1750, formed the central unit of an imposing civic group, of which a building originally put up as a tabernacle for George Whitefield was also a part. The interior of the latter was modified in the 1750s to fit it for collegiate use by the newly organised Academy of Philadelphia. Nearby stood a two-story brick market house and an assembly hall built by the Freemasons. The completion of the Philadelphia Hospital in 1756 testified further to the city's architectural maturity. The work of the Quaker, Samuel Rhoads, the hospital combined utility with grace of line. Although private house building failed to keep pace with the growth of population, some 1,500 new dwellings rose during the 1740s and 1750s. Furthermore, a contemporary noted, 'Additions, alterations, decorations are endless. Tis one eternal scene of pulling down and putting up.' The outward thrust of the city extended the built-up area for a mile along the Delaware. Some of the older tenements were crude little jerry-built structures, but well-designed two- and three-storey brick houses roofed in tile or slate redeemed the overall appearance of most sections. Benjamin Franklin's invention, moreover, added greatly to the comfort of the better-built houses when Philadelphians began to instal his iron fireplaces with exposed stove pipes that vastly increased the heat given into the rooms. Franklin himself, however, observed of his 'Pennsylvania Fire-Places' that 'the highest they ever raised my thermometer was to 56'.

Oddly enough, the architecture of the smallest of the Northern cities rivalled Philadelphia's. Perhaps Newport's limited expanse emphasised the beauty of her public buildings and the harmonious proportions of the mansions of her wealthy merchants. During the 1740s she spread out along the harbour's edge and up towards the crest of the hill where a half-dozen windmills rose against the skyline. But private building declined in the next decade: at the end of the French and Indian war the entire town consisted of only 888 houses, somewhat over 400 warehouses, and 15 to 20 churches and other public edifices. Her architectural fame nevertheless spread. It rested first on the 'Colony House', finished in 1743, but more largely upon the buildings designed by Peter Harrison during the next sixteen years. Yorkshire born, Harrison had shipped as cabin boy on a vessel of his brother's in 1937 and seven years later married into Newport's most aristocratic family. Presumably that connection brought him his first commission—to design a lighthouse for an island in the harbour. His skilful adaptation of the Palladian style which the Earl of Burlington had employed at Bath and John Wood used in Bristol found immediate favour in New England. Fort George in Newport harbour, the Doric-columned Redwood Library, the brick Market House and, perhaps his most admired piece of work, the synagogue for the Congregation of Sephardic Jews, anticipated the classicism of Thomas Jefferson and set a pattern for American urban architecture that endured for nearly three-quarters of a century.

This proliferation of handsome public buildings in the colonial towns was an expression of civic pride shared by all citizens, but it received special impetus from the mercantile aristocracy. In fact, some of the buildings were put up at the expense of rich individuals or groups of merchants. For although war cost some men their fortunes, the two decades preceding the Peace of Paris brought the colonial merchants as a class to the apogee of their power and prestige, and many of them enjoyed the role of patrons of the arts and public benefactors. They gave generously to eleemosynary and educational institutions like the Philadelphia Hospital and New York's King's College. Their patronage brought into being public concert halls, organs in churches, and singing societies, and opened careers to young artists such as the son of a tobacco-shopkeeping mother, John Singleton Copley, who painted over forty distinguished portraits of Boston notables before he was twenty-four. In the 1740s and 1750s rich men followed the example of the Philadelphia Junto in founding library companies, and their support encouraged a lengthening list of colonial publications. Interested in the progress of science, some of them undertook investigations of their own in the fields of botany, medicine, or astronomy.

Having helped bring their communities through the years of urban adolescence and the turmoil of war, in 1760 when hostilities shifted to the Caribbean, these men anticipated freer commerce, greater profits, and broadened fields of activity as expansion of settlement inland accelerated with the elimination of French and Indian interference. Merchant families whose ships had dominated colonial trade for a century, planters whose tobacco, rice, and indigo had enriched both themselves and the mother country, and gentry who had invested on a large scale in marine insurance, city or country real estate, or, in defiance of parliamentary edicts, home manufactures saw no reason to doubt that they would continue to control the economic growth of British America and assume an increasingly important role in its administration. Among them were some newly rich men who had exploited personal connections with royal officials to obtain fat government war contracts and who now expected the Crown to acknowledge their services by political preferment.

These expectations proved ill-founded. Even before the Peace of Paris in 1763, business depression overtook the colonial cities. Peacetime deflation inaugurated the commercial reverses, but troubles were worsened by the British ministry's adoption of a tightened imperial policy, new customs regulations, rigid enforcement of old, new forms of taxation imposed by Parliament, and the Currency Act invalidating the issues of paper money which colonials had used for years. The venality of customs inspectors was particularly hard to bear; inasmuch as they profited directly from every cargo confiscated, they trumped up charges that enabled them to multiply seizures and fines. If the merchants engaged in overseas trade felt the pinch at first, it soon squeezed shopkeepers and artisans, caused unemployment among common labourers, and eventually affected the agricultural countryside. Nor, to the disappointment of aspirants to lucrative posts in the colonial service, did Americans usually receive the appointments that ensured big fees along with social recognition in official circles; most of those positions went to younger sons of the English peerage and London-bred friends of the ministry.

The cities' mercantile leaders showed considerable resourcefulness in adjusting to the new economic conditions. To lessen the drain of specie to London and Liverpool, importers and craftsmen in the Northern towns turned to various home manufacturing enterprises. In a search for new fields of trade, Boston, New York, and

Philadelphia firms sent agents to establish commercial connections with Quebec and Montreal, Newporters developed markets in West Florida and westward along the Gulf coast, and Charlestowners looked to East Florida. New towns joined with old in enlisting aid from provincial legislatures to build roads into the back-country. Here and there groups of private citizens put money into improving highways. Enlarging internal trade went far towards offsetting losses in shipping to the mother country and Europe. In the mid-1760s the main road from the west into Philadelphia was crowded week after week by companies of 100 or more 'Conestoga' wagons. Developed by Pennsylvania craftsmen along Conestoga creek, these huge 'ships of inland commerce' were sturdy, canvas-covered, four-wheeled farm carts. Each wagon required two to four specially bred horses to draw it when loaded; the teamster sat on an outboard or astride the off horse. In 1766 one Philadelphia firm sent 600 pack horses and a wagon train laden with goods valued at £50,000 over the mountains to Pittsburgh; there boatmen loaded the merchandise on to bateaux and rafted it 1,800 miles down the Ohio and Mississippi to New Orleans. New England townsmen in trading with the back-country still relied upon ox-drawn carts or sledges in winter, but the number of vehicles and the miles of highway passable at all seasons increased steadily. In the Carolinas the network of wagon roads built into the interior benefited not only Charles Town but planters and isolated farmers in the uplands.

Thus, in spite of disturbing fluctuations, trade and manufacturing gradually expanded. While the five leading cities together added over 30,000 inhabitants between 1760 and 1775, fifteen secondary towns reached a size that by then standards ranked them as urban communities. Baltimore, for example, on Chesapeake Bay above Annapolis, grew from a village of 200 people in 1752 to nearly 6,000 and was offering Philadelphia serious competition as a market for the farm products of the fertile Susquehanna River valley. New Haven on the Connecticut shore of Long Island Sound numbered some 8,300 souls in 1775, nearby Norwich and New London 7,000 and 5,300 respectively, and seven other seaports from Portsmouth, New Hampshire, to Savannah, Georgia, had several thousand each. Furthermore, testifying to the success of efforts to link the interior with the seaboard, four inland towns—Albany in New York, Hartford and Middletown in Connecticut, and Lancaster in Pennsylvania—grew to the proportions of small cities. Large-scale immigration after the Peace of Paris accounted for much of this increase, although only some of the newcomers stayed in the towns. A great many of the Palatines and Scotch-Irish who landed in Philadelphia or Charles Town quickly moved on westward and southward to stake out homesteads in the hinterland.

While the towns strove to meet the demands for housing, schools, poor relief, and all the needs that recurrent hard times and insufficient local tax money intensified, people in the rural areas looked with mounting disfavour on the cities. Farmers' and frontiersmen's dependence on the seaports for European manufactured goods and markets for their own produce and furs failed to dispel their belief that they were victimised by wealthy city merchants. The antagonism of the country bumpkin towards the city slicker mounted from the late 1750s onwards, a hostility that would endure for two hundred years until automobiles, telephones, radio, and television largely obliterated basic differences between rural and urban life in America.

Some of the rising resentment sprang directly from economic problems created by the new imperial policies. As currency restrictions caused colonial importers trouble in meeting their obligations in London, merchants and town retailers limited the credit they allowed buyers in the back-country. While city tradesmen imprisoned for debt strained the capacities of provincial jails, debtors in rural areas attributed their woes to the greed of town exploiters. The growing secularism of the towns also offended the countryman to whom religious orthodoxy was still a rule of life; he looked upon the mob violence occurring with mounting frequency in the cities as proof of their depravity. The fact that the excitements they offered irresistibly drew young men from the farms added to the distrust felt by conservative country dwellers:

> Yankee Doodle came to town
> Riding on a pony
> Stuck a feather in his hat
> And called it macaroni.

Yankee Doodle keep it up,
Yankee Doodle Dandy,
Mind the music and the step
And with the girls be handy.

The popular ballad hinted at the countryman's view of the wicked city and showed the townsman's amused disdain of the farm boy.

City dwellers, on the other hand, had a grievance against their country compatriots because of the disproportionate representation in the provincial assemblies and the tax burden that consequently fell upon townspeople. Although the disparity was not new, townspeople objected to it with fresh passion in this era of stress. New Yorkers, who constituted a fifth of the population of the entire province and who paid a third of its taxes, had two seats out of twenty-seven in the Assembly; Philadelphians, entitled by the taxes they paid to have at least seven representatives in Pennsylvania's councils, had two; and in other towns the imbalance was only less pronounced. Though the situation in Charles Town evoked relatively few complaints, the silence apparently sprang from the realization that the tidewater gentry who controlled the Assembly neglected with bland impartiality the wants of both town and hinterland. In the Rhode Island legislature country debtors taxed their Newport creditors by means of frequent issues of paper money. Boston vainly begged the Massachusetts General Court for tax relief. Although the town meeting and town autonomy over purely local affairs enabled the New England cities to handle their municipal problems without constant interference from the General Courts, there, as elsewhere, the inequitable incidence of taxation set city against country.

Nor did unanimity obtain within the cities. In the lower ranks of urban society jealousy of the rich and well-born had long been in evidence, but it strengthened in the hard times of the 1760s and 1770s. Cleavages deepened between creditors and debtors and between merchant aristocrats and the middle-class intelligentsia, while differences sharpened between the increasingly powerful Anglicans and members of dissenting sects. Partly obscured by those not unfamiliar opposing alignments, a split began to appear also in the top stratum of colonial society. Undeterred by the failure of the Crown to honour colonials, men ridden by ambition to occupy a leading place in the new British imperial hierarchy taking form under their very eyes, stood out against fellow citizens who believed that British America must develop untrammelled by Old World trappings and by laws that Tory squires enacted in a Parliament oblivious of the needs of a vigorous young country beyond the Atlantic. Seemingly healed for a time by conciliatory measures, the breach between the advocates of an ultra-colonialism and proponents of a fully fledged British-American partnership became irreparable early in the seventies. By 1774 a small group of would-be aristocrats in the provincial capitals was looking to the day when the Crown would create a titled American nobility. Where 'the middling sort' and the 'poorer sort' stood was never in question, if only because the colonial press staunchly opposed special privilege.

The printers of this period might well be called the single most influential body of men in the colonial world. Twelve weekly English news sheets and, in the vicinity of Philadelphia, one or two German-language papers kept people informed about political issues, religious controversies, and scientific developments. The newspapers carried, for example, detailed accounts of new experimental work on electricity in which Benjamin Franklin was the foremost innovator. Franklin, arch exponent of the artisan's potentialities, inspired other 'mechanics' to conduct experiments. As he trained scores of young printers, often lending them money to start their own establishments, the number of newspapers, broadsides, and pamphlets rose steadily. Distinctly members of the middle class and yet men of affairs with a general knowledge of the world, the printers served as the arbiters of colonial taste, disseminated European ideas, and promoted programmes aimed at bettering municipal conditions. Through an intercolonial correspondence reminiscent of that of fifteenth- and sixteenth-century European merchant princes, they moulded public opinion from New Hampshire to Georgia in a fashion that the self-styled 'best of the better sort' could not do. Renewed official attempts in the 1750s to impose censorship on the press had merely heightened its influence, as men of substance as well as the 'middling sort' and the 'lower orders' perceived that any such curtailment of colonial liberty would injure them all.

Troubles in Boston brought matters to a head. No other one town had suffered commercially so severely during the wars in the 1740s and 1750s. In that 'Metropolis of Sedition', as one official called her, 'the Democratick Thermometer' rose in 1765 'some Degrees above the Boiling Heat' in protest against parliamentary taxation, oppressive customs rulings, and Royal Navy impressment of Massachusetts seamen. Colonial shipmasters now avoided the port lest they lose their crews to press gangs and part of their cargoes to overzealous customs inspectors. The quartering of British regulars in the town in 1768 was the first of a series of events that focussed the eyes of the colonial world upon the Massachusetts capital. Next came the so-called Boston Massacre when soldiers on guard duty, in dispersing a mob of boys who had been throwing snowballs and taunts at them, killed five of the rioters. The famous Boston Tea Party followed in 1773, and, as punishment for dumping the tea into the harbour, the closing of the port. A 'Journal of Occurrences' in the colonial press reported every detail and magnified numerous lesser episodes, but the accounts could scarcely exaggerate the want and misery of Boston's working classes during 1774 or the rising anger of her moderates. On a lesser scale and with less 'mobbish' resistance to British authority, similar 'occurrences' disrupted life in other colonial towns.

By 1775 a majority of the city gentry and Southern planters had thrown in their lot with the American commonalty. They saw nothing but a pusillanimous notion of safety to attract them to a scheme of things characterised for over a decade by a colonial civil list from which they were barred, by nepotism or appointments of obsequious, unscrupulous self-seekers, by Anglican suppression of the majority, and by a flaunting of riches and position in the face of popular distress. The time had passed for negotiating with a blind British ministry, arrogant Crown officials, and colonial sycophants. Patriots perceived that America could never be a replica of the Old World, that strong albeit ill-defined libertarian forces were stirring in the colonial cities, that a new ethos was emerging. Disciples of the Enlightenment, they felt impelled to share in the making of a new social and political order. That need not mean, in fact most of them believed it must not be allowed to mean, a 'democratical' form of

government. Dismayed though they were at the organised mob
insurrections in the seaports, faith in the ultimate victory of reason
and justice soothed their fears of the excesses of the 'Sons of Liberty'.
Shortly after the signing of the Declaration of Independence, Lord
Howe, commander of His Majesty's forces in the rebelling colonies,
noted that 'almost all of the People of Parts and Spirit were in The
Rebellion'.

The eight turbulent years of the American Revolution brought
the cities of the defiant self-proclaimed nation a variety of troubles.
Farmers and homesteaders on the frontier had their share also, but
at least they escaped the worst of the chaos caused by British army
occupation of the principal cities. With the exception of Charles
Town, each of the former colonial capitals lost much of her population between 1775 and 1776. From a town of 40,000, Philadelphia in
a year dropped to fewer than 22,000, New York from 25,000 to
5,000, Boston from 16,000 to 3,500, and Newport from 11,000 to
5,300. The cost to the country was beyond estimate. Leaders not
enrolled in the Continental Army scattered hither and yon, returning to their homes only when British troops withdrew. The Committees of Correspondence who had inspired the assembling of the
Continental Congresses contained scores of shopkeepers and tradesmen who thus were as guilty of treason as their social betters.
Indeed the middle classes, whose resourcefulness and talent for
organisation Tories consistently underestimated, were scarcely less
responsible than the merchants for launching the revolt and carrying
it through. Certainly all patriots recognised the truth of Benjamin
Franklin's pithy comment at the time of the signing of the Declaration of Independence: 'We must all hang together or we'll all hang
separately.'

Supplying the Continental Army put heavy demands upon all
patriots. In the seaports, as soon as British troops evacuated for
action in the field, shipyards resumed the building of privateers;
rope-walks, sail lofts, and smithies fitted them out. Rum distilling,
virtually an essential industry, continued, while city printing establishments published the newspapers and pamphlets equally sustain-
ing to public morale. Perhaps the want of sound money caused the
greatest anxiety. The Continental Congress had to rely chiefly on

levies on the thirteen states which were all too frequently in arrears, but promises of land grants to men who enlisted in the army served as a substitute of sorts. For two generations after the war an American byword 'not worth a Continental' recalled the rapidly depreciating value of the paper money issued between 1776 and the late 1780s. Probably only the loans negotiated in Paris and French arms, troops, and naval vessels made victory possible.

When peace and acknowledgement of American independence came in 1783, spiritual exhaustion, debts, and the collapse of trade engulfed the new nation. War had impoverished the country. Along the waterfront of the ports, ships without cargoes lay tied up at the wharves while unemployed seamen wandered through the streets. Americans, no longer British subjects, were now excluded from trade with the British West Indies and the profitable 'long haul' from the islands to England; direct shipments to Britain involved paying heavy duties; neither Whitehall nor continental European governments permitted purchase of American-built ships; and such surplus foodstuffs as the United States could supply were marketable only in the French, Dutch, and Spanish islands. Retail shops shut up for want of customers. The Congress of the Confederation was all but helpless. The states, each trying to get revenue for itself, had erected customs barriers that further inhibited trade. Each of the thirteen had drafted a state constitution, set up courts, and held yearly or biennial elections for legislative and administrative offices —governmental machinery patterned upon modifications of colonial models. But state officials and state laws appeared unable to revive commerce, or even maintain order. If the situation was less desperate than it seemed to its victims in the 1780s, it nevertheless called for statesmanship of a high order to handle constructively. To reopen familiar channels of trade, find new outlets for American products, and establish American credit in a fashion calculated to create and preserve a sound currency constituted a triple task as formidable as it was essential to national survival.

The experience necessary to solve problems of this magnitude resided preponderantly in the city merchants and lawyers, abetted by Southern planters whose association with the colonial commercial world had been close. These men realised that, before the United

States could expect to negotiate favourable trade treaties with foreign nations, the Congress of the Confederation must have funds with which to settle national debts contracted during the war. Land was the one obvious asset. But until the states ceded to the nation their claims to the western lands stretching beyond the mountains to the Mississippi, the 'Father of Waters', Congress could not capitalise on that resource or redeem its promises to Revolutionary veterans. New York, the first to withdraw its claims, acted before the war was over, but not until 1786 did the last of the states with valid claims relinquish them, leaving the Congress of the Confederation free to set up territorial governments for that inland empire and, through sales of small parcels of the national domain, open it section by section to orderly settlement. With the enactment of the Northwest Ordinance of 1787 the United States achieved a solid basis for a kind of national land bank.

Meanwhile delegates from the states convened in Philadelphia in the summer of 1787 in an endeavour to halt internal commercial rivalries by forming 'a more perfect union'. The Constitution, painstakingly hammered out, was submitted to the Congress that autumn, then went to state conventions for ratification, and won the endorsement of nine of the thirteen states in 1788; the remaining four states ratified it later. Even before the new federal government was fully organised, the common market created by the constitutional prohibition on interstate customs duties was quickening trade, and before the first federal Congress met in New York late in 1789, the sale of government land in the Northwest Territory was bringing money into the United States Treasury. Import duties soon added to those sums.

Internal conflicts nevertheless had run strong. Massachusetts had had a taste of class warfare when farmers, oppressed by debts and mortgage foreclosures in the western part of the state, had taken up arms in protest at the concentration of power in the hands of the rich and well-born in the seaport cities, especially Boston. State authorities had suppressed the insurrection and then made some concessions—a moratorium on private debts, a reduction of taxes, and an arrangement for payment in kind on state levies—but among 'the poorer sort' distrust lingered on. Nor was the antagonism of

hinterlanders towards city dwellers and the struggle between the
have-nots and the haves confined to Massachusetts. Several state
legislatures controlled by back-country representatives voted to
move state capitals to rural areas: Charles Town, renamed Charleston, lost out to Columbia in the South Carolina uplands; somewhat
later, Philadelphia had to yield to Lancaster, and New York to
Albany, while Newport had to alternate with Providence as capital
of Rhode Island. All state constitutions contained a property qualification for holding office, and most of them applied it to voting for
presidential electors, representatives in Congress, and members of
the upper house of the state legislature, but no two states had
identical requirements. Manhood suffrage obtained in Vermont;
Virginia, South Carolina, and Georgia denied the elective franchise
to free Negroes; New Jersey permitted women to vote. Some states
established easier qualifications for voting in city and town elections
than those specified for national and state. The town meeting still
functioned in New England cities, but elsewhere local government,
like state and national, was at best representative rather than
democratic.

Although the urban population was scarcely a twentieth of the
rural, the cities continued to dominate the economy, and within the
towns, old and new, the merchants still held the reins. In Philadelphia, Boston, and New York, private banks chartered before the
mid-1780s strengthened their hands, and when Congress chartered
the Bank of the United States in 1791 to handle federal funds, the
shareholders were primarily city merchants. After 1785, from the
Northern seaports and the upstart Baltimore, a few merchantmen
undertook the long voyage around the Horn to the northwest
Pacific and the Hongs of China. If the ship returned safely, the two-
and-a-half to three year venture might net shareholders as much as
250 per cent on their investment. The slave trade, on the other hand,
was in the doldrums, for planters in the South were uncertain about
what crops they could raise profitably. And the poverty of the
agrarian South affected adversely the coastal trade of Northern
cities. Indeed no section of the young republic felt utterly secure.
Still, the vast stretches of virgin lands to the west held abundant
promise. Moreover, in keeping with a provision of the Constitution

that called for the creation of a national capital in territory exclusively under federal jurisdiction, in 1790 Congress passed the so-
called Residence Act which specified a location on the Potomac
River on land ceded by Maryland and Virginia. As surveys of the
site moved forward and the plan for the city of Washington took
shape, Americans' faith in their future deepened.

3

'MANIFEST DESTINY'

In the seventy years after the formation of a strong federal union a nation of some 3,172,000 whites and three-quarters of a million Negro slaves living east of the Mississippi River, chiefly along the eastern seaboard, increased to 31,443,000 people spread from the Atlantic to the Pacific coast. 'Our manifest destiny to overspread the continent' and to extend the blessings of Democracy to all the hemisphere was a boastful political pronouncement of the 1840s, but to most Americans it expressed a simple truth. The confidence embodied in the doctrine of 'Manifest Destiny' was, to be sure, a gradual growth. It was budding at the end of the eighteenth century, suffered intermittent malnutrition until 1815, and reached its peak in the 1850s before the 'irrepressible conflict' over slavery checked it. While the westward thrust of the frontier fed it, its strength derived also from the burgeoning urban centres and the tide of industrious immigrants flowing into them. Here 'in time's noblest Empire', wrote an exuberant journalist in mid-century, the vital forces of the nation lay in her cities, old, new, and still unborn, cities 'outrivaling in splendor as in magnitude, all which past ages have produced'.

Although the vast stretches of virgin land were the young nation's greatest resource, in the 1790s commerce was still the fulcrum on which American prosperity rested. Importers in the seaport cities and merchants in inland towns had to furnish many of the supplies homesteaders needed in settling new territory, just as farmers with surplus produce to sell had to ship it to the nearest town. Markets made accessible by ocean-going ships, river craft, or wagons on overland highways were as important to the tillers of the soil as to city and town merchants. And as settlement spread westward, new towns sprang up. Until the end of the War of 1812, commercial relations with Europe, to be sure, hung in rather precarious balance. The Jay Treaty, negotiated with Britain in 1794, opened the British West Indies to small American vessels for a limited period of time and so removed some of the difficulties that had beset American shipping interests. Along the waterfront of the seaport cities activity immediately quickened. But the Royal Navy's impressment of American sailors and French search of American ships on various pretexts continued to imperil American foreign trade and eventually led to war with Britain. Yet in the face of all hazards the commercial and financial position of the United States gradually strengthened. The growing power of particular cities may help to explain that phenomenon.

The emergence of Baltimore as a major commercial centre offers one illustration. A town of 6,000 at the outbreak of the Revolution, she more than quadrupled her population in the next twenty-five years. Nature gave her advantages. Unlike vessels sailing from the older American ports, her ships bound for the West Indies or Southern coastal depots on leaving the mouth of the Patapsco River sailed the protected waters of Chesapeake Bay for a hundred miles before reaching the open sea and so had a safer as well as a shorter run than from Philadelphia, New York, or New England. Her location on the upper Bay, moreover, made her the logical marketplace for the wheat that farmers were beginning to raise in western Maryland. In the 1790s, even before the state legislature granted her a municipal charter, her merchants set about improving upon nature. They built roads that enabled them to snatch from Annapolis much of the tobacco trade of southern Maryland. They dredged the mouth of the Patapsco, filled the marshland adjoining, and put up warehouses and wharves along the extended waterfront until her docking facilities rivalled New York's. Shipbuilding thereupon expanded. When war with France threatened in 1798, Baltimore shipyards built two of the six frigates commissioned for the newly created United States Navy. Meanwhile, with an eye to obtaining maximum cargo space for such bulky commodities as barrels of flour and hogsheads of tobacco, shipwrights designed and built roomy-bottomed merchantmen, special rigged and carrying huge spreads of canvas that offset the bottom-heavy construction and guaranteed sailing speed. Before the end of the eighteenth century, ship-owners, combining the functions of banker, marine insurer, and trader, established regular runs to Bremen, where they landed tobacco and, on the return trip, brought back German emigrants anxious to farm in the back-country or ready to ply their artisans' skills in the enterprising young city. As mountains of wheat and rye poured in from an ever-widening farm belt in western Maryland and from the rich Pennsylvania countryside drained by the Susquehanna River, flour milling and distilling rye whisky became highly profitable. Use of the mechanised system newly devised by the talented Oliver Evans of Philadelphia enabled millers to turn out fine-grade flour in quantity at relatively low cost. And with the rye whisky came that innovation, the cocktail. By combining food processing, ship-building, foreign and domestic trade, and well-advertised services to German immigrants, Baltimore made herself by 1810 the third city of the United States, surpassed in size and wealth only by New York and Philadelphia.

A second example of mounting economic stature was Providence. British occupation of Newport during the Revolution first caused the transfer of most of Rhode Island's foreign trade to the city at the head of Narragansett Bay, and although Newporters recaptured control of the African slave trade in the 1780s, their neighbours kept the lead in other transactions. The constitutional prohibition on slave imports ended Newport's commercial power in 1808. By 1810 Providence ranked second to Boston among New England cities and fifth among all American cities. Cotton manufacture contributed to that achievement. For in 1790 Samuel Slater, having slipped secretly out of England carrying in his head the essential details of the Arkwright spinning frame, undertook to build from memory cotton-spinning machinery for two Providence merchants. The Rhode Island shop opened the next year. Its immediate success spawned several other cotton factories in southern New England and inspired Providence capitalists to invest in further textile and ancillary enterprises, notably the manufacture of specialised tools and machines. The city thus became one of the first manufacturing centres in the country.

American cotton spinning, in its infancy before 1815, could scarcely have developed at all had Eli Whitney's invention of the cotton gin in 1793 not turned Carolina and Georgia planters to raising short-staple, green-seed cotton. The consequences of the device that transformed an otherwise useless fibre into the principal export staple of the United States were far-reaching. From Charleston and Savannah a steadily mounting tonnage of cotton moved to Liverpool and to the few New England towns where spinning mills operated in the early years of the nineteenth century, but neither Carolinians nor Georgians took charge of financing or shipping the crop. By 1810 virtually all enterprising Southerners were dedicating their energies to acquiring more land and more slaves to clear and plant it to cotton; they willingly let Northerners, chiefly New Yorkers, carry on the selling arrangements. Charleston, the acknowledged capital of the Cotton Kingdom, soon ceased to think of herself as a commercial city at all, as she basked in the role of residential and cultural centre of the plantation country. Southern indifference to 'money-grubbing' constituted New Yorkers' opportunity. Their ships picked up cotton in Charleston or Savannah, traded it in England for British goods wanted at home, carried the cargoes to Manhattan, and then transhipped the wares that would bring a top price in the South. The system, though not fully worked out until after 1815, was taking form in the first years of the new century, and, abetted by liberal New York state auction laws, helped make Manhattan the greatest commercial centre in the United States. Furthermore, planters' increasing concentration upon cotton raising enabled Philadelphia and Baltimore merchants to sell them bread-stuffs and New Englanders to market salt fish for the South's multiplying cotton-field hands. Nor is it perhaps wholly fanciful to suggest that New Haven owed some of her growth to the fact that there Eli Whitney opened his shop to build his patented gins and there carried on experiments in manufacture by the 'interchangeable system' which he applied in the early years of the nineteenth century to small-arms making. That method formed the basis of the modern assembly line.

The migration of settlers into the trans-Alleghany West mean-while brought river ports into being on the Ohio. During the 1780s Virginians and North Carolinians had moved in such numbers into the 'dark and bloody ground' south of the Ohio that Kentucky had a large enough population in 1792 to enter the Union as the fifteenth state; in that interval Louisville on the river where rapids and falls required portaging of cargoes grew from a tiny trading post into a booming town. Simultaneously, as New England and New Jersey land companies bought up military land warrants and started settle-ments on the north bank of the great stream French explorers had called '*La Belle Rivière*', Pittsburgh at the head of navigation took on special importance. There householders who had made the arduous journey over the mountains into western Pennsylvania prepared for the more perilous trip downstream. Some of them, observing the demand for blacksmiths, carpenters, harness makers, and other craftsmen in this outfitting centre, chose to stay in this busiest com-munity in the transmontane United States. Others, driven by the restlessness that already characterised Americans, moved on to homestead and form new towns in virgin country. Of the new settlements in the Northwest Territory none made swifter progress than Cincinnati; the cluster of cabins about the United States fort three hundred-odd miles downstream from Pittsburgh turned into a prosperous trading post, and, when the army garrison was trans-ferred in 1803, the newly incorporated town had 800 inhabitants and Ohio had won admission to the Union.

At that moment President Jefferson's purchase of the Louisiana Territory from Napoleon vouchsafed still faster growth. With the old French and Spanish city of New Orleans near the mouth of the Mississippi in American hands, shipments of produce from the farms multiplying about Cincinnati could reach eastern markets by water; the lumber lashed into rafts on which river boatmen usually floated the bulky cargoes down the 1,500-mile stretch also com-manded good prices in New Orleans. Homesteaders of the fertile Ohio country in need of a shipping centre and ambitious Cincinnati merchants together formed in 1803 the Miami Export Company for collective buying and selling, an instance of an unusual and long-enduring co-operation between town and country. Among other mutual benefits, the arrangement provided a credit system badly needed in a region where hard money was scarce. Small wonder that within a decade Cincinnati's population of 1803 tripled, brickyards, tanneries, and slaughterhouses edged the town, wharves and taverns lined the river front, lawyers' shingles began to protrude from doorways, and Presbyterian preachers and Methodist circuit riders sought halls in which to save the souls of townspeople preoccupied with the rewards of the world about them.

The Louisiana Purchase rather alarmed arch conservatives on the eastern seaboard who foresaw that the addition to the United States of a vast region of unknown extent reaching north-westward to the Pacific must dilute the power of the original thirteen states. New England merchants were especially apprehensive; their trade, already suffering from the constant westward migration of families from the hill farms of their hinterland, was likely to shrink still faster as shipments sent through New Orleans mounted in volume. For different reasons the 'Creoles' of New Orleans were as displeased as the Yankees. An admixture of Breton, Norman, French Canadian, émigrés from the French and Spanish West Indies, Canary Islanders, refugees from Acadia and from San Domingo after the slave insurrection of 1796 drove white men from the island, the Creoles resented their involuntary new status as American citizens. They so disliked the boisterous river boatmen from the States that they relegated 'les Americains' to a separate section where they would obtrude as little as possible upon householders of the 'Vieux Carré'. French-speaking traders from St Louis, the 'gateway to the West' a thousand miles upstream, alone received a welcome. Newcomers familiar with Eastern cities, if charmed by New Orleans' exotic quality, were none the less critical of conditions along her crescent-shaped Mississippi River front—the planking laid over the earthen dykes, the levees, to serve as wharves, the lack of warehouses, and streets deep in mud. Only during business transactions did the French-speaking Orleannais deign to associate with the English-speaking intruders. Those transactions, however, were profitable. Foreign trade that expanded from $5 million a year to $15 million in a decade, a few successful experiments in refining sugar from Louisiana cane, the legal importation of slaves before 1808, and organised slave-smuggling thereafter, all enriched the divided community.

Other than New Orleans and the Carolina and Georgia cotton ports, whose shipments to Liverpool were too important to Lancashire to be subjected to British interference, all the seaboard cities faced commercial losses before and during the War of 1812. New Orleans largely escaped them because the Purchase treaty had given French and Spanish ships entering there special concessions and because the British postponed the siege of the city till December 1814; an early American victory quickly followed by news of peace exposed her to a scant month of hardship. The Northern ports, on the contrary, were first hampered by an embargo of 1807 and later by Nonintercourse acts by which President Jefferson attempted to force European recognition of American rights; the major shipping centres generally ignored the prohibitions but were nevertheless handicapped by them. Curtailed commercial activity meant hard times not only for merchants but also for shopkeepers, clerks, sail makers, foundry men, and dock hands. When Congress declared war in 1812, New York and Baltimore shipmasters took out letters of marque and reprisal, but Boston, already crippled by earlier reverses, chose to carry on a clandestine trade with Nova Scotia which Britain encouraged. New England townsmen, in fact, were desperate enough to plan a withdrawal of their states from the Union. Fortunately peace halted the plan. Salem never wholly recovered, but in the new era that dawned in 1815 Bostonians gradually recaptured prosperity by putting mercantile capital into cotton manufacture and developing new mill towns inland where water power was available.

With the coming of peace, a wave of euphoria swept the country. The next quarter of a century, marred though it was by two 'panics', depressions caused chiefly by orgies of speculation and over-rapid expansion, brought astonishing growth to America's cities, and, as the wilderness retreated before the onslaughts of homesteaders, new towns and embryo cities arose wherever obvious geographic advantage and individual enterprise dictated. The introduction of steamboats to the western waters hastened this transformation of the frontier.

By 1806 Oliver Evans had developed and was manufacturing in

Philadelphia lightweight, high-pressure steam engines suitable for propelling ships; Robert Fulton's steam ferry was operating on the Hudson River the next year; and steamboats slowly came into use elsewhere along the coast, but the hazardous navigation on the inland rivers delayed their appearance on the Ohio and Mississippi. About 1811 Evans opened a shop to fabricate his steam engines in Pittsburgh, where competent blacksmiths gave the enterprise a solid foundation at this strategic point of transfer from overland routes to the western rivers. But not until 1818 after Cincinnati began building steamboats did they become a mainstay of river commerce. For the shipper of wares upstream from New Orleans the steamboat offered tremendous savings in time, risk, and cost. Instead of the seventy-eight-day record for a barge poled up to Cincinnati, steam transport in the 1820s cut the trip time to about twenty-five days. Pittsburgh and Cincinnati machine shops which produced engines soon branched out into making sugar presses and machines for a dozen other purposes. Every town along the Ohio and Mississippi benefited from the steamboat. St. Louis's trade with New Orleans doubled, and by 1835 the Louisiana port, with commerce valued at some $54 million, had a larger volume of exports than New York City. On the inland seas of the Great Lakes steamers were relatively few until completion of the Erie Canal in 1825 gave impetus to settlement of northern Ohio and the territory beyond.

Like steamboats, New York state's 'big ditch' and the canals dug by other states and private companies envious of the success of Erie Canal spurred city growth. New York City profited more directly and more largely than any other one community, for, as the 350-mile waterway begun in 1817 pushed westward from the Hudson at Albany towards Buffalo on Lake Erie and towns sprang up along its course, produce from the adjacent countryside moved eastward. over the completed stretches to the Hudson and thence to Manhattan, and shipments of goods went from the port to the interior. While Buffalo, western terminus of the canal, grew into a city, the canal traffic secured permanently to New York the commercial leadership she had wrested from Philadelphia, enlarged her financial resources, and helped make 'Wall Street' a term synonymous throughout the United States with monetary power. Pennsylvania's imitative attempt to link Philadelphia and Pittsburgh by a combination of canal and land transport cost taxpayers $14 million without effecting comparable results, just as the money sunk into the Chesapeake and Ohio Canal along the Potomac westward from the national capital through Maryland neither yielded investors satisfactory returns nor created new centres of trade. In Ohio, on the other hand, a network of canals built to feed into the Erie fostered the growth of secondary towns lying between the Ohio River and Lake Erie:

A French visitor describing the birth of towns in the early 1830s wrote:

In the anthracite region [of eastern Pennsylvania], in the manufacturing districts of the North East, along the New York canals, and in all parts of the West, a traveller often has an opportunity to see the process of building towns. First rises a huge hotel with a wooden colonnade, a real barrack . . . the landlord being, as a matter of course, a general, or, at least, a colonel of the militia. The bar-room is at once the exchange, where hundreds of bargains are made under the influence of a glass of whiskey or gin, and the club-room, which resounds with political debate, and is the theatre of preparations for civil and military elections. At about the same time a post-office is established; at first the landlord commonly exercising the functions of postmaster. As soon as there are any dwelling-houses built, a church or meeting house is erected at the charge of the rising community; then follow a school-house and a printing press with a newspaper, and soon after appears a bank to complete the threefold representation of religion, learning, and industry.

Had the Frenchman travelled as far afield as the tip of Lake Michigan he might have added colour to his tale by describing the effects of land speculation on city building at Chicago. The mushrooming growth of Chicago within four years from a village of 350 inhabitants in 1833 to an incorporated municipality of 4,100 began with 'canal fever'. In 1827 the Illinois state legislature had obtained a federal land grant to help finance a waterway from Lake Michigan via the Chicago River to the south-westward-flowing Desplaines and so into the Mississippi. But the meagreness of settlement in northern Illinois had discouraged potential investors. The dreary-

C

looking huddle of shacks about Fort Dearborn at the toe of Lake
Michigan held little promise of a commercial future until a young
lieutenant of the United States Army during a campaign against the
Indians in 1832 observed the magnificent fertility of the treeless
prairies and in 1833 persuaded Congress to vote money to dredge
the Chicago River and make a safe anchorage for lake shipping.
Practically overnight the projected Illinois and Michigan Canal
looked not only feasible but commercially all-important. When the
federal land office in Chicago opened the auction sale of lots along
the canal's surveyed course, competitive bidding among the specu-
lators drove prices up to fantastic figures. As digging on the canal
began in 1836, a second sale brought in $1,041,344 for 186 canal lots
within Chicago's limits. A local newspaper bragged that Chicago
real estate was rising 'in value at the rate of *one hundred per cent per
DAY*'. People flocked to the town to 'get in on the ground floor'.
The town became a city early in 1837. The balloon collapsed a few
months later, after President Jackson's 'Specie Circular' required all
federal Land Offices to accept only gold and silver in payments on
government land purchases. Panic swept the country.

The immediate sequel to Chicago's story shows how courage,
tenacity, and imagination could offset folly and greed. As the panic
spread, Illinois state banks closed, credit dried up, prices plummeted,
merchants went bankrupt, and work on the canal stopped. In the
new city, land valued a few months earlier at $10 million dropped
to a scant $1.25 million. Ruined by the disaster, a number of residents
moved away, generally westward with the wagon trains of homesteaders heading for greener fields beyond. But stouter-hearted
Chicagoans refused to admit of defeat. Two insurance companies
issued certificates of deposit which bankers accepted in local business
transactions, so that the scrip soon acquired the validity of legal
tender. Craftsmen and merchants were then able to carry on by
making and selling household equipment and agricultural tools to
transients bound for the open prairies. And when farms nearby
began to be productive, Chicagoans shipped the surpluses east by
lake steamer—thirty-eight bags of wheat in 1838, nearly 600,000
bushels five years later. Before the end of the 1840s, small boats were
moving through the newly opened canal from Lake Michigan to

the Mississippi, and, while real estate speculation resumed, Chicago engaged in another bold venture—railroad building.

Baltimore was the first American city to put faith in rail transport. In 1827 her bankers, after hearing a careful description of English experience with a railway, concluded that locomotives and iron tracks laid over the mountains and into the Ohio Valley would be the best means of capturing a share of the western trade which the Erie Canal was diverting to New York. Within five months Baltimoreans had prepared a plan, obtained a company charter, raised $3.5 million of capital, and engaged a competent engineer to start construction of the Baltimore and Ohio Railroad. Before the enterprise was five years old, freight was rolling into Baltimore in a volume that gave her undisputed commercial control of most of Maryland, and by mid-century, when the iron tracks reached the Ohio Valley, the Chesapeake Bay port, as an outlet for Western produce, had attained a position that only New York and New Orleans could challenge. In 1857 the Baltimore and Ohio entered Cincinnati.

Other Eastern cities were not slow to follow Baltimore's example, even when they had good water ways at their doorsteps, for, unlike canals and rivers, railroads were usable at all seasons of the year, the speed of delivery offset the relative cheapness of shipping by boat, and, most important of all, land routes could reach areas commercially unapproachable by water. So, the Erie Canal notwithstanding, at the end of the 1820s New Yorkers undertook railroad building, Philadelphians and Pittsburghers, backed by the state legislature, began work on the Pennsylvania Railroad, and Massachusetts men embarked on building the Boston and Albany. Bostonians who had invested money in textile mills and machine shops located near the coast at the fall line of New England rivers at once saw the advantages of widening the geographic range and hence the profitableness of their manufacturing ventures. While the Boston and Albany tracks crept mile by mile across the state, Boston capital simultaneously developed mill sites, factories, and new mill towns in localities formerly too inaccessible to warrant exploitation. Two Massachusetts towns illustrated the changes a railroad could cause. In one prosperous community townspeople refused a right of way to the

Boston and Albany; company engineers thereupon chose a route through the hamlet of Worcester. By 1850 the former was shrinking, while Worcester was emerging as a commercial centre; by 1860 Worcester had become one of Massachusetts' chief cities.

Without abandoning the river trade, in the mid-1840s Cincinnatians also started overland lines to connect with those from the eastern seaboard and with St Louis. At the end of that decade St. Louisians began promoting a railroad through Missouri and mapping out a scheme of extending rails to the Pacific. Chicagoans by then had already tasted the satisfaction of watching wheat pour into the city over the first few miles of tracks on the Galena and Chicago Union Railroad. That success, made possible by persuasive company officials who had canvassed shopkeepers and farmers of the vicinity to induce them each to buy a share or two in the enterprise, launched Chicago on a railroad building career unequalled elsewhere in the world. By 1854 the rails of the Illinois Central were nearing the Gulf of Mexico, two lines from the east ran into the city, and during a single month the Chicago and Rock Island carried nearly 170,000 passengers and 49,736 tons of freight over its hundred miles of tracks laid between the lake port and the village on the upper Mississippi. A year later Chicago had 10 trunk lines and 11 branch lines; 96 trains daily were puffing into her depots. By 1860 she boasted 109,000 residents.

As the mounting demand for iron for steamboat engines, locomotives, and railroad tracks caused an expansion of the iron industry, several Pennsylvania towns grew to the dimensions of cities. From the eighteenth century onwards the ores in eastern Pennsylvania, the skilled smiths, and the mercantile capital available in and about Philadelphia had made the Quaker city and her satellites a centre of American iron making. Here and to the north-west around Harrisburg, the state capital after 1812, and at Scranton, iron-masters in the 1830s and 1840s were introducing improved methods of fabrication —substituting rolling mills for trip-hammers, refining the puddling process, and, as the charcoal resources of the area ran low, developing a method of working the iron on hearths out of contact with closed, mineral-fuel-burning furnaces. Expensive equipment and the necessity of employing a considerable work force in order to in-

crease output had the effect of concentrating the industry in relatively few localities. When Pittsburghers learned how to use coke
derived from the rich bituminous coal deposits in their immediate
vicinity, the new process enabled them to challenge Eastern competitors. Locomotive works, opened in the early 1830s in Philadelphia,
were exporting their product to Europe before 1840, and by 1860
the two largest concerns, together with a Patterson, New Jersey,
firm, built 258 of the 470 locomotives turned out in the United
States. Rail manufacture was more widely spread, but Pittsburgh's
rolling mills were a main source in the 1850s. When the completion
of the Sault Ste Marie Canal in 1855 permitted the rich iron ores
of Michigan's Upper Peninsula to move by water from Lake
Superior to Lake Erie and thence by special ore cars to Pittsburgh,
the 'Black City' secured to herself a dominant position in American
heavy industry. First the steamboat and then the railroad set the
nation on a course of industrialisation.

Although the 1840s and 1850s saw cities multiply and grow at a
faster rate than in any other period of national history, the attraction
of virgin land awaiting occupancy continued to draw men westward. While Eastern cities sometimes felt drained by that migration,
St Louis, located just below the confluence of the Missouri and
Mississippi, made the most of her opportunities to outfit families
setting out for the Oregon country and traders bound for Santa Fe
in Mexican territory. With the settlement of the Oregon boundary
question, the annexation of Texas in 1845 and, consequence of war
with Mexico, the addition to the national domain of all the territory above the Rio Grande from the Texas boundary to the Pacific,
the westward movement gained fresh momentum. And Eastern
cities, like the rest of the country, shared in the excitement over
the discovery of gold that set the 'forty-niners' on the trails to the
California gold fields. At San Francisco, where a magnificent
natural harbour enabled ships to deposit prospectors and supplies for
burgeoning mining towns, a city of 50,000 grew up in a matter of
months. Enterprising Bostonians shipped prefabricated frame
houses to the Golden Gate, and other Eastern cities pushed trade
with the West Coast. For the next seventeen years talk of a trans-
continental railroad filled bar-rooms in San Francisco and bankers'

offices in Eastern and Mid-western cities until it became a reality after the Civil War. In the meantime, the railroad age, created by city enterprise, was forcing the South to re-examine her position.

For fifty years the Cotton Kingdom of the Deep South had showed little enthusiasm for city enterprises and city building. Cotton fields were more important than marketing centres in plantation owners' eyes, and only planters' opinions carried weight in the southernmost tier of states lying east of Texas. Small towns and crossroad villages could manage day-by-day transactions; when the time came to sell the year's cotton harvest, Northerners' ships, docked at Charleston, Savannah, New Orleans, and the few newer ports along the Gulf coast, could handle the crop and on the return voyage bring back European luxuries and American manufactures and foodstuffs. The interstate slave trade whereby the upper South, especially Virginia, sold its surplus field hands to the cotton country required little city-based organisation. Before 1850, when Congress forbade the domestic slave traffic in the capital, Maryland and District of Columbia traders were allowed to use the Washington city jail to house their human wares in transit. Few Southerners were troubled by their dependence upon Northern credit and Northern merchandise or saw reason to develop their own banking and commercial centres until railroads threatened to make the recently acquired Southwest a Northern preserve. 'It is owing to the lack of a great commercial city in the South', wrote Hinton Helper of North Carolina in 1857, 'that we are now annually drained of more than One Hundred and Twenty Millions of Dollars!' If the South had abandoned slavery and, instead of building up 'mammoth cities at the North', had spent its resources on developing its own commercial centres, 'how much richer, better, greater, would the South have been today! . . . Almost invariably do we find the bulk of floating funds, the best talent, and the most vigorous energies of a nation concentrated in its chief cities.' Although Southerners set themselves to building railroads in the late 1850s, city promotion was slow. If slave-owning Texans accepted Helper's argument, sheer space worked against the ranchers and farmers scattered over the plains. Austin, the state capital, the settlement about the army post at Fort Worth, and Galveston, the principal port on the Gulf, were still small towns in 1860.

Exhilarating as the expansion of the urban frontier was to its beneficiaries, few cities, old or new, achieved an atmosphere of stability or a stable business class. Men opened retail stores or shops for processing raw materials, made or lost money in their enterprises, and then, driven by a hunger for something new, moved on to another community. Whatever his source of livelihood, the successful townsman managed a speculation, not a business. Anthony Trollope, in describing the Mid-western cities he visited in 1861, noted: 'Men build on an enormous scale, three times, ten times as much as is wanted . . . Monroe P. Jones, the speculator, is very probably ruined, and then begins the world again, nothing daunted. . . . He is greedy of dollars with a terrible covetousness; but he is greedy in order that he may speculate more widely.' Nation-wide panics only briefly deterred the Monroe P. Joneses. Despite the griefs of 1837, by 1841 urban real estate prices were renewing their climb to dizzy heights, and, after over-expansion brought on the panic of 1857, again city promoters forgot about it within a year or two. Yet, as Trollope pointed out, their greed more often than not left the cities in which they exercised it somewhat richer, at least supplied with buildings for new arrivals to occupy. And new arrivals there always were.

Nine cities, five of them seaports, three of them river or lake ports, and one, Brooklyn, independent suburb of New York, had each over 100,000 inhabitants in 1860, another twenty-five more than 25,000 each, and some four hundred at least 2,500 each. All told, 6,216,500 Americans ranked as city dwellers, nearly a fifth of the entire population in contrast to a twentieth in 1790.

Municipal services, however, failed to expand proportionately as problems caused by swelling urban populations became progressively more acute. For a generation after 1790, it is true, the administrative methods of the colonial era sufficed. Nor did the advance of the social revolution marked by the adoption of white manhood suffrage in state after state seriously affect city government before the end of the 1820s. Boston, for example, reluctantly abandoned the town meeting scheme in 1822 when more than 41,000 inhabitants made the system unworkable, but under the guidance of her first mayor, Josiah Quincy, later President of Harvard College, the transition from town to city went smoothly. In big cities and small, greatly enlarged electorates chose mayors, councilmen, and lesser officials from lists of property owners; men of standing in the community accepted public offices as an honour and, according to their lights, performed their duties conscientiously. In the newer cities of the interior also, charters modelled on those of the older seaboard communities left the affluent in charge. But as the pressures of Jacksonian democracy led states and cities to drop the property qualification for holding office, the character of city administrations changed, frequently for the worse, for the levelling process that wiped out class distinctions in politics simultaneously weakened the sense of *noblesse oblige* among well-educated gentle folk.

The 'excessive development of the democratic principle', as de Tocqueville termed the phenomenon in Cincinnati, was especially pronounced in the cities with large numbers of foreign-born in their midst. By the 1850s New York, Philadelphia, Boston, and a half-dozen others were beginning to come under the sway of political bosses supported by 'ward heelers' who aligned the votes of newly naturalised citizens and the poorest of the native-born. The deliberate withdrawal of the 'first families' from civic responsibilities partly explains this incipient new order. Furthermore, men caught up in the excitements of accumulating riches in land speculation, railroad building, banking, and industrial promotion were loath to give time to municipal problems. In the post-Civil War era that washing of the hands would become more general and the consequences far more obvious.

Politics on the state and national level, on the other hand, interested all classes of urban society except newly arrived aliens. The most affluent citizen was unlikely to refuse to run for the state governship if his party caucus selected him or, after the discarding of that method of nomination, if influential party members supported his candidacy at the primaries. He might also be willing to campaign for a seat in the House of Representatives or in the state legislature, inasmuch as that body elected United States senators. As city electorates broadened, national party organisation tightened; the concentration of city population made party loyalty at once easier to establish and more necessary for election victories. Yet issues primarily urban in character gave rise to a new splinter party in the early 1850s—the anti-foreign, anti-Catholic Know Nothing or American party, which proposed to halt immigration into the United States.

Although many of the British-born and north-German immigrants who arrived in the early years of the century took to farming, later comers, especially the poorest of them, more often settled in the cities. Day labourers from the southern counties of Ireland in the 1820s and 1830s dug most of the canals and laid the roadbeds of American railways, while uneasiness stirred in and about Boston and New York lest those alien Roman Catholics, many of them illiterate and speaking a heavy brogue or no English at all, submerge native Americans. Still the tide continued to rise, and, after the potato famine struck Ireland in 1847, unskilled and semi-skilled Irish labourers and their families thronged the Eastern seaboard cities. Within four or five years Irish factory hands were supplanting the native farmers' daughters in Massachusetts cotton mills. English and Scottish immigrants escaped most of the hostility that greeted the Irish, but Germans encountered some of it, particularly wherever they formed a distinct colony perpetuating their own language and social customs. In Northern cities where the Know Nothing party was born, anti-foreign, anti-Catholic sentiment reached a pitch that produced street battles fought with brick-bats, stones, and name-calling. Boston Know Nothings set fire to a Roman Catholic convent, and a group in Washington dumped into the river a block of marble the Pope had sent to the capital to emplace in the Washington Monument. But anti-Popery and the wish to preserve the purity of Anglo-Saxon America proved an insufficient basis for party unity as the crisis over slavery developed. By 1856 a good many Know Nothings had either shifted to the infant Free Soil party or returned to the disintegrating Whig or the Democratic camp.

Native-born, English-speaking Americans themselves still faced resentment from the Creoles of New Orleans. The Louisiana legislature attempted to cut the Gordian knot in 1836 by creating three separate municipalities within the city. The 'Vieux Carré', the American quarter, and a third on the outskirts each elected its own officials, set up its own taxing system, and printed its own municipal currency,

'shin plasters', with which to pay its obligations. The Second Municipality was thus free to pave streets, spend its harbour fees to maintain public schools, and undertake other services which the French-
speaking First Municipality considered extravagant folly. The split,
however, created more problems than it solved, and when bank-
ruptcy threatened in 1852, all parties agreed to revert to a single city
administration. Manifestly the best efforts of everyone were needed
to combat the ravages of cholera, malaria, and yellow fever in a
city built on swamp-lands and subject to the periodic wash of high
tides over the levees along the river front.

While geography and climate imposed peculiarly severe problems upon New Orleans, no city of the antebellum period evolved
adequate safeguards for public health. Philadelphia set the example
of building public water works in the first decade of the century,
and nearly seventy cities followed that course when urban promoters
discovered that piped water would boost real estate sales; in other
places private water companies constructed reservoirs, pumping
stations, and mains. But the pipes rarely extended beyond the most
expensive residential areas. Elsewhere wells and pumps in the public
squares had to serve, and, inasmuch as improper drainage and faulty
sewer systems, if they existed at all, frequently contaminated the
wells, epidemics of dysentery, typhoid, and less deadly diseases
were common. If in the worst yellow fever years of the 1850s
New Orleans set a sorry record with 25,000 deaths out of a population of some 116,000 people, mortality in big Eastern centres year
after year was scarcely less appalling.

Housing shortages contributed to the high death rates. Congestion
was inescapable as long as most people had to rely on shanks'
mare to go and come from their work, but when street railways
appeared in New York, Philadelphia, and Boston in the 1850s, the
horse cars moved too slowly to be of much help. The method New
Yorkers early adopted to accommodate the swarms of newcomers
landing at their docks was to sub-divide rooms in old mansions
located in downtown areas from which the well-to-do had moved to
fashionable new sections. By mid-century warehouses also had
turned into tenements with five or six families jammed into a single
twelve by fourteen foot room. Tales told of the overcrowding in

the 1820s and 1830s ceased to shock conscientious citizens when they read of conditions described in the report of the state Tenant House Commission of 1857. Want of supervision, that report indicated, had permitted great cities to become 'great sores, . . . excrescences upon the body of created things'. While New York's explosive growth made matters worse there than in other places, slums were appearing in Philadelphia, Boston, Baltimore, and several inland cities.

Casual attitudes towards regulations essential to orderly living were the rule. Where ordinances like those of colonial Boston forbade throwing slops into the streets, householders in nine cities out of ten now honoured the law chiefly in the breach. To the disapproving astonishment of foreign ministers, even in the national capital swine were the principal public scavengers. In fact, few public services improved over those established in the colonial era. Volunteer hose and hook and ladder companies still carried on the fire-fighting but often displayed more zeal about fighting each other than about extinguishing fires. Cobble-stoned streets threaded the business districts and fine residential areas; dust or mud, according to season, dominated the rest. Although Baltimore installed gas lamps on her streets before 1816, city fathers there and everywhere deemed moonlight sufficient illumination save on cloudy nights. In the darkness the violent crime and petty misdemeanour that Sir Robert Walpole's London 'Bobbies' had learned to keep in check flourished in American cities. The lawlessness of American society which later generations would trace to the frontier had its roots perhaps equally deep in the fierce competitiveness of the American city. Certainly the constables and the small bodies of uniformed police created in the 1850s were unable to preserve peace and order.

Even more distressing was the prevalence of abject poverty in the midst of plenty. Poorhouses and orphan asylums maintained by charity and public monies could not cope with the increasing numbers of desperately needy people. If Elizabeth Pickering's comment of 1740 on the indolence of the 'poorer sort' in Southern communities had some bearing on conditions in all American cities a century and more later, the explanation neither satisfied philanthropic citizens nor suggested any immediate way out of the dilemma. The most generally accepted solution lay in educating the younger generation.

The ideal of free schooling for every child at public expense had spread since the seventeenth century. Within the Northwest Territory it became announced national policy when the Ordinance of 1787 set aside for public school support one section of land out of the thirty-six comprising every township. Almost universally, it is true, townspeople early dissipated that resource by selling the land instead of leasing it, but throughout the states carved from the Territory tax-supported schools gradually came into being in every town and city. In all the Eastern states north of the Mason-Dixon line and in Maryland, Delaware, and the District of Columbia as well, by the 1840s city school systems, however faulty, were receiving public money, and citizens elected or appointed to school boards were supervising its spending while they mapped out curricula, hired and fired teachers, and built schoolhouses. That the quality of educaton thus provided usually fell below that offered in private schools was on the whole less important than the fact that the great body of American public opinion upheld the principle of free education at a time when neither Britain nor any nation of continental Europe except Switzerland paid it even lip service. City dwellers in the slave-holding South were less wedded than Northerners to the principle and far less ready to act upon it. Yet St. Louis inaugurated a system in 1853 that not only gave children an exceptionally thorough grounding in elementary subjects but carried pupils through four years of high school at public expense. The 'Athens of America', Boston, could herself do no better.

If the amenities of city life in contrast to rural were less evident than in the eighteenth century, the city still 'formed the substance of American civilisation. It was in the cities that men by mutual imitation changed toward what they considered improvement.' While urban architecture usually suffered from the tastelessness of the Monroe P. Joneses, public buildings in a great many cities continued to achieve a dignity and grace of line that vied with the best in contemporaneous Europe. Philadelphia, birthplace of much of the finest in the United States, managed to preserve the central core around Independence Hall from the inroads of the early Victorian era. The national capital at Washington also testified to American search for beauty. Like other foreigners before and after him, Charles Dickens poked fun at the 'city of magnificent distances' where rubbish-strewn vacant lots and unsightly shanties marred the effect of imposing white-stone-pillared federal office buildings, but discerning persons, however unenthusiastic about the classical architectural style, perceived grandeur in the concept and could envisage its possibilities. At a later date Englishmen who admired the Crystal Palace and the Victoria and Albert Museum were scarcely in a position to ridicule the turreted red-brick Norman castle erected in the 1850s for the Smithsonian Institution at Washington.

In domestic architecture in the 1830s and 1840s North and South alike fell under the spell of the Greek Revival. Self-schooled carpenters learning from books of drawings generally built the handsome houses that rose along the Gulf coast, in New England, in Baltimore, Cincinnati, and scores of cities between and beyond. In the old section of New Orleans the imprint of eighteenth-century French and Spanish rule was still visible in the stuccoed walls and iron grill work, arches, balconies, and inner courts with fountains and statues half-covered by roses and vines; the newer American quarter seldom succeeded in reproducing that charm. The Spanish influence was even clearer in Texas towns and the trading posts of New Mexico. Although jerry-built monstrosities cropped up in all cities, particularly in the newest and rawest, civic pride in time impelled men to put up more substantial, and, by then standards, more beautiful buildings. The rows of houses standing shoulder to shoulder flush with the streets in colonial towns rarely had counterparts in newer cities. There, fenced yards, sometimes adorned with flower beds, ordinarily surrounded private dwellings.

Yet it was not the all too dubious external beauty of American cities that drew people to them. As in colonial days, it was the seemingly infinite variety of ideas and experiences available there. The city alone opened up the world of art. Only there could the gifted musician find the inspiration of hearing finished concert performances, and only there could the aspiring young painter find masters to train him. The artist might start his career as a self-taught itinerant, gaining experience from painting trays, shop signs, and portraits of small-town dignitaries, but sooner or later he sought instruction, or patrons, or both in the city. So Chester Harding, portraitist of three Presidents and a score of other notables, began as a sign painter, tried his hand at portraits in rural Kentucky, and then, after two months' study in Philadelphia and a sojourn in St Louis, opened a studio in Springfield, Massachusetts, and in Boston, where a 'Harding craze' brought him fame. Although many a small town displayed a few curios in its local lyceum hall, picture galleries and museums containing that rarity, sculpture, existed only in the largest, most sophisticated centres.

Furthermore, despite the philosophers and writers who in gathering about Ralph Waldo Emerson gave Concord, Massachusetts, a unique place in the American literary world, the nation's foremost men of letters were generally city-dwellers. Few attained the enduring distinction of New York's James Fenimore Cooper and Washington Irving, or of Baltimore-resident Edgar Allan Poe, and few won the more ephemeral popularity of Boston's Oliver Wendell Holmes, but fewer still sought rural quiet in preference to the stimulus of the city. About 1830, books donated to a local athenaeum began to form the nucleus of the public library that was soon to become the symbol of urban culture. When the Boston Public Library opened its new building in 1861, it contained 100,000 volumes which any citizen might read for the asking. By mid-century in laboratories on half a dozen college campuses scientific investigations were moving forward, while in Washington the Smithsonian Institution, founded upon a bequest from an Englishman, James Smithson, 'for the increase and diffusion of knowledge among men', published reports and data relating to basic research. The findings, thanks largely to the press, commanded far greater attention in the cities than in relatively isolated spots, even though lyceums multiplied in villages and small towns from the 1830s onwards. Intellectually curious young men inevitably gravitated citywards. The force attracting them exceeded that exercised upon their forebears by the eighteenth-century cities.

City diversions, however, varied little from those of the colonial era, except in so far as nineteenth-century pastimes were open to all classes of society. In the Mid-west, Mrs Trollope's *Domestic Manners of the Americans* noted, revival meetings took precedence over other forms of entertainment, including her own waxworks display of 'The Infernal Regions', but the genteel widow avoided Cincinnati's waterfront taverns and saloons where carnivals regularly staged for river boatmen combined gaiety with some true native artistry. While the impecunious never gave or attended formal balls, in every city they might frequent dance halls and public gardens to listen to brass bands or accordions and fiddlers. Choral societies also came into vogue, particularly in cities like Cincinnati, St Louis, and Baltimore with large German-born populations. When Jenny Lind, the 'Swedish Nightingale', toured the United States in the 1850s, it was a very poor person indeed who did not spend money to hear her.

New York had by then taken the undisputed lead in theatrical productions. Then, as now, no eminent British actor would dream of omitting an appearance on Broadway while he was on tour in the United States. He naturally played in Boston as well, for he could expect the 'Brahmins' to provide discriminating audiences. Chance and the depth of his curiosity about the rest of the country might determine his other bookings. They were more likely to include Baltimore and several mid-western cities than Philadelphia, for, after the federal government moved in 1800 to the new capital at Washington, the Quaker City had reverted to mild disapproval of the stage, and interest in the theatre was slow to reassert itself. In the 1840s along the Ohio and Mississippi rivers show boats began to ply, tying up at wharves at river ports up and downstream to give a potpourri of melodrama and music. In many an inland town, however, travelling circuses were a greater attraction than the performances staged by barnstorming troupes of actors. For to much of rural America the theatre, that urban product, epitomised at once the wickedness and fascinations of city life.

The godlessness that small-town and country people attributed to the city notwithstanding, the conscience of the United States worked in urban communities as fully as in less populous areas, and generally

with more effect. Abolitionists in the 1830s set up their presses in
the big cities, although the evils of slavery were most clearly visible
on Southern plantations. Negroes, slave or free, made up large
segments of the population in New Orleans, Washington, Baltimore, Richmond, Charleston, and a few smaller Southern cities.
Lesser percentages caused anxiety in St Louis and in free Ohio's
Cincinnati; elsewhere in the North, familiarity with the operation
of the 'peculiar institution' derived from newspaper stories, pamphlets, lectures, and sermons. Conservative Northerners disliked
and feared abolitionist radicalism with its preachments of civil dis-
obedience, but newspapers like William Lloyd Garrison's *The
Liberator* survived attempts to suppress them. Harriet Beecher
Stowe's *Uncle Tom's Cabin*, inspired by several years spent in Cincinnati, appeared serially in 1852 in an abolitionist paper published
in Washington.

Unhappily the plight of free Negroes received relatively little
attention even from anti-slavery crusaders. Since Southerners
looked upon freedmen as potentially dangerous agitators likely to
incite slave uprisings, Southern state laws declared it a crime to teach
Negroes to read; Southern municipal black codes not only subjected them to an oppressive surveillance but limited the occupations
open to them. Nor, except in Vermont, did they win full American
citizenship anywhere in the North. No Northern community
welcomed coloured immigrants. In the 1830s Cincinnati chose to
enforce rigidly a state law designed to restrict a Negro inflow by
requiring from every coloured person a $1,500 bond for good be-
haviour and denying coloured children admission to the public
schools. Although the ruling was later relaxed, in all border cities
east and west some hostility to 'free people of colour' endured.
Skilled Negro craftsmen in Philadelphia and several other Northern
centres might make a fair living, but only where their numbers
were comparatively few could they count on freedom from petty
persecution.

Yet in the 1850s the voice of protest over slavery mounted steadily
in volume and intensity. It sounded loud in the Northern cities
even while business leaders strove to temper its force. Rising passion
swept the country in 1860. In the presidential election that autumn,

one scholar has observed, 'urban support for the moderate candidates, both North and South, reveals the city as a potential deterrent to the Civil War'. Public opinion in the urban centres nevertheless joined with small town and agrarian countryside in producing the explosion of 1861.

4

THE IMPACT OF INDUSTRIALISATION

1860–1910

The transformation of the United States from an agricultural to a predominantly industrial nation within a half-century and the accompanying rise to a position of world power was directly associated with accelerating urbanisation. Which came first, the hen of mounting industrial strength or the egg of increasing urban influence, may be arguable, but the fact of profound change remains. It proceeded by fits and starts.

The four years of civil war expanded heavy industry and precision manufacture but cut a hole into the earlier pattern of steady commercial growth. Post-war adjustment was uneven: an upsurge of energy in Northern cities and the West, lassitude verging on paralysis in the defeated South. Panic and prolonged depression struck the entire country in the mid-1870s without greatly weakening the control 'robber barons' had begun to exercise over the national economy. During the next thirty years that stranglehold tightened and then relaxed under reformers' attacks and the challenges of a middle class gradually revitalised by multiplying occupations. In the interim, railroad building, mining, manufacture of heavy machinery, inventions, and the spread of mass production techniques increased national wealth manyfold, while the concentration of population in cities proceeded concurrently with the peopling of the Western plains. Belief that the millions of acres of free fertile land which had once seemed inexhaustible had shrunk almost to the vanishing point in the mid-1890s forced Americans to reappraise their future. In 1910 farmers and villagers still outnumbered city dwellers, but the inhabitants of the 2,405 municipalities spread across the continent were rapidly overtaking the rural population. And to both country and city the frontier had become a romantic memory.

In the late winter of the black year 1861, Northern businessmen and moderates in the South still hoped for a compromise that would bring back into the Union the nine states that had already withdrawn to form the Confederacy. But in April when South Carolinians fired on the American flag flying over Fort Sumter in Charleston harbour, the conflict between the agrarian 'slavocracy' and the largely commercial, industrialising North became indeed irrepressible. While most of the South jubilantly hailed independence and noted the effects of runs on Northern banks, the dwindling stocks of raw cotton in New England factories, and the disruption of trade in commercial centres whose principal markets had lain in the plantation country, angry Northerners told themselves they would soon lick the rebels. Yet despite the superior material resources of the North, not until the Union succeeded in making the blockade of Southern ports effective and a dozen bloody battles had thinned the ranks of the men in grey did Southern communities feel the economic pinch acutely and the Confederate armies betray their weaknesses. By then casualties and calls for new enlistments were creating manpower shortages in the North also.

Government orders for uniforms, blankets, shoes, railroad equipment, and munitions eventually restored industrial activity in much of the North. Pittsburgh alone built a half-dozen new foundries in a single year; before the war was over, Philadelphia had 200 new factories in operation. Traffic in foodstuffs, draft animals, and fodder for army camps increased the volume of railroad freight and enriched contractors in Chicago and other cities with productive agricultural hinterlands to tap. Shipbuilding at the United States Navy yards in Boston, Brooklyn, and Philadelphia also expanded from 1862 onwards. The Union capital at Washington, source of government contracts, a hospital centre, and the main forwarding

point for supplies for the Army of the Potomac, doubled in population within four years; Richmond, the Confederate capital, was
similarly bursting at the seams before her capture in the spring of
1865.

Yet despite government contracts, industrial output during the
decade failed to rise at a rate comparable to that in the 1850s.
The production of pig iron, for example, which had increased by
17 per cent between 1855 and 1860, rose only 1 per cent during
the next five years. The miles of railroad track laid during the
war were less than half the total of 1855–60. Examination of long-
term trends in a number of other areas tells the same story. The
conclusion is hard to avoid that, in checking the expansion of
industry and the spread of transport, the Civil War retarded the
economic developments that had fostered urban growth in the
1840s and 1850s. In the social and ethical realm the costs were equally
high. While the abolition of slavery was an over-all good, the greed
and ruthlessness exhibited by many Northern entrepreneurs implied
that the war, so far from being a fight for human rights, had encouraged unscrupulous exploitation of the public. That spirit would
rule big business in the metropolitan centres for years to come. In
the South the desperate attempts at self-sufficiency produced little
but bitterness and the belated realisation that agriculture alone could
not support an independent nation, a lesson first put to use in the
1880s with the emergence of the 'New South'.

More immediately visible to city dwellers at the time were the
social changes the war brought in its wake. Although cheap immigrant labour was in demand, the influx from Europe declined between 1860 and 1865. Draft riots in New York and other ports of
entry deterred emigration from Prussia, whence rebels against
military conscription had fled in 1848, and warned off such Irishmen as were unwilling to leap from the frying pan of hunger in
the Old Country into the fire of the battlefront in America. Furthermore, battle casualties left families without breadwinners and forced
women to take up unfamiliar occupations even after government
pensions eased their lot. With that change in their home lives,
children roamed city streets and raised the rate of juvenile delinquency to alarming heights.

A still more baffling problem for the Union's border cities, Washington above all, was the migration of Negro field hands from the South into urban communities where there were no jobs for them. After President Lincoln's Emancipation Proclamation of January 1863, legally those from the rebel states were now free people at liberty to move about as they chose. Their illiteracy, their lack of skills suited to a city environment, and their all too frequent irresponsibility about their own future harassed their reluctant hosts even while their pitiable condition awakened sympathy. Here was the first wave of a tide that would recede at intervals in the years ahead but would sweep constantly higher in the twentieth century and from the 1930s onwards profoundly trouble every Northern metropolis. The squalor in which most of the penniless newcomers of the 1860s lived added to community health hazards and sent Negro mortality to peaks that led to an occasional prophecy that coloured people, manifestly unable to survive as freed-men, would soon die out as a race and thereby automatically eradicate race problems. Meanwhile, during and immediately after the war, city school boards, aware that school systems must educate the ignorant black invaders, wrung their hands over the cost but generally took no other action.

Virtually all municipalities had to shoulder new financial burdens. Not only did the cost of necessary services go up as inflation set in, but tax delinquence mounted and so reduced public revenue. Contractors for war supplies who reportedly were making fortunes were often slippery customers, adroit at evading the tax collector. After the first months of war, moreover, popular fervour for joining the Army wore off, and although states offered men bounties to enlist, mayors and councils in Northern cities struggling to meet draft quotas sometimes felt obliged to offer supplementary bounty payments. Every year of war lengthened the list of families in need of some form of public assistance.

Fortunately the United States Sanitary Commission formed in 1861 was able to help soldiers' needy dependents from time to time and to ease some of the anxieties families felt for their menfolk in army camps and hospitals. For the commission, sometimes called 'Lincoln's Fifth Wheel', supplemented the services of the undermanned, overworked Army Medical Corps by conducting sanitary inspections, reporting on shortcomings, and furnishing badly needed medical supplies. The Aid Societies that had organised in towns and cities throughout the Union in the first weeks of the war usually became branches of the commission. Sanitary fairs held in major cities raised money for ambulances, surgical supplies, medicines, and hospital equipment. This non-professional medical corps, composed largely of volunteers, was an antecedent of the American Red Cross.

For Southern cities difficulties multiplied inexorably; the tighter the Union Navy drew the blockade about Confederate ports, the greater the want. Union occupation of New Orleans, Mobile on Alabama's Gulf coast, and, for brief periods, inland cities within the Union battle lines subjected residents to humiliations, the commandeering of foodstuffs, and, now and again, confiscation of private property. Household slaves sometimes decamped to join the Union army, although plantation field hands were more likely to desert their familiar surroundings. By the end of 1864 Confederate currency had become all but worthless, city merchants rarely had goods to sell at any price, and Atlanta, Georgia's largest city and the principal railroad centre of the South, lay in ashes. In the capital at Richmond the improvised military hospitals were overflowing with wounded, and food was so scarce that even members of Jefferson Davis's cabinet had to dine sparingly. When the Confederacy surrendered the following April, all her cities and most of her countryside were utterly impoverished.

Victory, if a tonic to the North, brought with it heightened restlessness. While 'carpetbaggers' with Congressional blessing took themselves south to pick up bargains in railroad holdings, timber lands, and other potentially profitable property, men recently discharged from the Army looked uncertainly at their peacetime world. Scarcely a town but offered mute testimony to the costs of the war: the names of the honoured dead inscribed on the base of the stone effigy placed near the town hall frequently seemed more numerous than those left on the tax rolls. Thousands of young men anxious to blot out the immediate past chose to start life anew in a different setting—in a nearby city, in the recently discovered mining regions of the Rocky Mountains, or on land which the Homestead Act of 1862 now opened up free to bona fide settlers. Southerners ruined by the war and, as European immigration resumed, Scandinavians, Germans, Czechs, Irishmen, and Britons swelled the train of westward-bound homesteaders, mining prospectors, and families heading for they scarcely knew what. The chartering in 1862 of the long-discussed trans-continental railroad subsidised by federal land grants along the right of way gave the movement added impetus. Within three years of the day in 1869 when a golden spike driven into the ties in western Nevada marked the junction of the Union and Central Pacific railroads completing the links between east coast and west, three other trans-continental lines were beginning to push across the plains towards the mountain passes to California and the forested shores of the Northwest.

While the ensuing steady dispersion of population over a vast area seemingly should have stunted urban growth, the reverse was true. For just as river and lake ports and, more rarely, canal towns sprang up and turned into cities at strategic points along the inland waterways, so trading posts and construction camps along the railroads sometimes became permanent towns and, depending on location, developed into regional supply and marketing centres or headquarters for railroad maintenance. Whereas Eastern cities built railroads, in the West railroads built cities. Thus Omaha on the windswept prairies of Nebraska and Salt Lake City, Mormon capital on the high plateau of mountainous Utah, owed their urban dimensions to the Union Pacific Railroad. San Francisco, by 1869 a city of 150,000 inhabitants, attained permanent metropolitan stature upon becoming a major rail terminus. In somewhat similar fashion the Kansas Pacific Railroad transformed Kansas City from a small prairie 'cow town' at the great bend of the Missouri River into a busy city. Cattle driven over the trails from Texas could be slaughtered here during the winter months and the beef be shipped east by rail. When competition threatened at the end of the 1860s, local leaders forestalled it by building the first bridge over the turbulent Missouri and thereby winning mainline connections with St Louis and Chicago. As the introduction of refrigerator cars in the 1870s made meat packing a year-round business, Kansas City and Omaha, along with Chicago and St Louis, became the principal suppliers of beef for the United States and for much of Europe as well.

More than one Western town, it is true, had to haul herself up by her own rail straps, much as Kansas City did with her bridge. Denver, 700 miles to the west at the eastern base of the Rockies, was a notable example. She had started as a mining camp in 1858 when prospectors had found gold in the mountain valleys nearby, but when the Union Pacific chose a route through a pass a hundred miles to the north, Denverites, seeing their future at stake, organised a local company and built a branch line to connect with the transcontinental road at Cheyenne, Wyoming. Then, although the Kansas Pacific reached Denver that same year, ambitious citizens enlisted the support of Boston capitalists in constructing a narrow-gauge railroad southward to coal fields at Pueblo and thence a few years later into the high mountains where the discovery of rich silver deposits meant a profitable traffic in ore to be taken to Denver for smelting. At the same time, cattle ranchers on the high plains to the east and farmers who learned to irrigate the fertile but arid soil of the surrounding countryside found Denver their most accessible market and best source of needed supplies. The upshot was that while Cheyenne, railroad junction though she was, remained a small town, in the early 1880s Denver emerged as mistress of a region stretching over 500 miles in every direction.

Not only inland localities without navigable waterways but Pacific seaports, like Eastern ports before them, early recognised the importance of railroads to their futures. At the end of the 1860s when the first trans-continental line was creating a new boom in San Francisco, Seattle on Puget Sound in the far Northwest was little more than a logging camp of a thousand people. But, possessed of the best safe anchorage for ocean-going vessels between Golden Gate and the Canadian border, she already envisaged herself as the ruler in time to come of a mighty commercial empire based on lumber, farm products, and fisheries. To achieve that goal she knew she would need closer ties with the rest of the United States than coastal vessels from San Francisco or ships sailing round Cape Horn could provide. What a Massachusetts journalist said of Colorado in 1869 applied equally to Seattle: 'The two things she lacketh chiefly now are appreciation at the East and women . . . but the railroad will speedily fill the vacuums.' For the remote outpost in the wilderness of the Northwest the first gap took longer to fill than the second, for a handful of Civil War widows and young girls willing to risk the long voyage round the Horn and the matrimonial uncertainties ahead had landed, taken husbands, and raised marriageable daughters in the town before Seattle won the financial endorsement in the East that brought her a major railroad. Later two more railroads secured to her the regional hegemony she aspired to. Supplementing the prestige deriving from her inland trade, her coastal shipping, and a growing commerce with the Orient came salmon canneries and, with the Gold Rush to Alaska in 1898, a huge business in outfitting miners.

Throughout the era of railroad building, the spreading networks, in making some towns into cities, relegated others to insignificance. Villages, towns, and small cities fought for the privilege of being on 'the main line'. The losers, even those with good water transport facilities, usually faced the alternative of withering on the vine or developing industrial enterprise that would ultimately draw a railroad to them. Yet, as Cheyenne, Wyoming, discovered, trains passing through were no guarantee that a town would wax great. Unless she had paying freight to fill cars daily she was likely to turn into a way station at which trains stopped only on special signal. In the 1870s, moreover, the system adopted by the major railroads of charging more for the 'short haul' than for the 'long haul' left many a small city a satellite of bigger neighbours. Her best hope of enhancing her position lay in the proverbial scheme of building 'a better mouse-trap', a course that a surprising number of young cities followed successfully. Thus Waterbury, in the 1840s a small town in western Connecticut where button makers had acquired special skills, turned herself into the brass centre of America. Similarly, Hershey, Pennsylvania, founded by a small candy company, attained a place so secured by the excellence of the chocolate bars she produced that neither the manufacturer nor the community ever needed to advertise.

In so far as the introduction of new manufacturing processes and the development of new products accounted for the transformation of industrial towns into cities, the failure of mining communities to follow that pattern was logical. The extractive industries continued to use the time-honoured pick and shovel for the basic work, although elevators in deep shafts and ore cars on rails in the tunnels were commonplace in coal, iron, and copper mines. The refining took place elsewhere, and miners drew their supplies from the nearest processing and shipping centre. Around the multiplying plants of heavy industry, on the contrary, concentrating population converted many a small city into a big and, measured in terms of the time, many a big city into a metropolis. Pittsburgh exemplified that kind of change when her iron-masters introduced the Bessemer process and began to make steel rails. Possessed of the first steel mills in the United States, the Black City grew like a sooty weed. And along with steel came such innovations as heavy steam-powered cranes and clam scoop shovels for unloading ore boats, and drills for oil wells.

Oil launched Cleveland on her successful industrial career. Thus half a dozen years after 'Drake's Folly' of 1859, when a so-called crackpot demonstrated how to pump petroleum from north-western Pennsylvania's underground caches, Cleveland on Lake Erie established oil refineries. These, under the directing hand of John D. Rockefeller, put the city in control of the American refining industry before the end of the 1870s. Already a terminal point for Great Lakes ore boats and the foremost commercial city of northern Ohio, Cleveland established herself as an industrial metropolis within a single generation. When the Standard Oil Company introduced pipe lines, she held her lead in oil processing. Minneapolis arrived at metropolitan status by the slightly different route of developing a new method of milling wheat. In 1860 little more than a village market for Minnesota farms along the upper reaches of the Mississippi, she seized her opportunity when farmers of the region took to raising spring wheat, a hard-kernel variety adapted to the severe climate of the northern plains, but difficult to grind into high-grade flour. Experiments in the mid-seventies with roller grinders such as Hungarians used in central Europe enabled Minneapolis millers to produce flour of a quality that quickly captured

Eastern markets. As that success encouraged farmers of the northern prairies to increase their wheat acreage and railroad builders to extend new lines across the northern tier of states, Minneapolis became the flour capital of the United States, outstripping the older milling centres at Baltimore and St Louis. Several companies later moved their mills to Buffalo in order to ship their output by Erie Canal as well as railroad, but by then Minneapolis was producing farm machinery and serving as a distributor of goods to all of Minnesota and neighbouring states. In every part of the country some cities similarly emerged from obscurity by developing a speciality based upon a local asset—papermaking in western Massachusetts, where the chemical properties of the Connecticut River contributed to a notably fine product, brewing in Wisconsin's largest city near hop farms whose German settlers endorsed the Schlitz advertisement of 'the beer that made Milwaukee famous', and cotton-seed oil in Memphis, Tennessee, adjacent to the most productive cotton plantations of the South.

Inventions also spurred urban growth. The sewing machine, patented in the 1840s, first contributed to the industrial rise of Bridgeport, Connecticut, where it was manufactured, and, when war contractors in New York put it to large-scale use, gave the ready-made clothing industry its start with Manhattan as its headquarters. In the early 1870s Thomas Edison's experiments gave birth to the electrical industry, which soon endowed Schenectady in upper New York state with special importance as the home of the General Electric Company. Four or five years later, factories making Alexander Graham Bell's telephones spread from Boston to a score of other cities. While plants turning out the newly patented typewriter multiplied in New England, the National Cash Register put Dayton, Ohio, on the industrial map. Furthermore, contrary to the general assumption that the assembly line first appeared in the American automobile factories of the early twentieth century, meatpackers introduced at the Chicago stockyards in the 1870s what one historian has called the 'disassembly line', a moving belt that carried the carcasses of hogs or steers one after another past a line of workmen each of whom performed a single task of dismemberment until perfectly butchered meat dropped off into containers at the end.

And, Chicagoans boasted, the only part of a hog not converted at the stockyards into a saleable by-product was its squeal.

Cheap immigrant labour, whether European, French Canadian, Mexican, or Oriental, provided the means of expanding some towns into cities and enlarging established manufacturing centres. While Northern and Mid-western communities drew upon European peasants and 'habitants' from Province Quebec, on the West Coast, despite a law of 1882 denying Chinese free ingress, coolie labour supplied a bottom layer of workers that exerted a downward, if indirect, effect upon industrial pay rates. In the 'New South' of the 1880s cheap native-born labour served the same purpose when Northern capital began to convert a number of communities in the cotton belt into textile towns. North Carolina 'hill-billies', Georgia 'crackers', and South Carolina 'poor whites' moved from impoverished farms into factories built by Northern money and initially run by Northern superintendents and overseers. In the south-eastern Appalachian coal and iron regions, it was again Northern capital and poverty-stricken whites from the up-country that built the foundries and steel mills that created the city of Birmingham, Alabama. Whites also manned most of the machines in New Orleans rice mills and sugar refineries, but here Sicilians who entered the United States through the Louisiana port became the main source of unskilled factory labour. Nowhere in the Deep South were Negroes permitted to work as factory hands alongside white people. 'Niggers' did the draying, the yard work, the 'roust-about' or stevedores' tasks, and menial jobs of cleaning and tidying up. After the turn of the century when 'black gold' spouting from oil wells in the Southwest brought industrial plants to the region, Mexican day labourers paid at minimal rates performed the heavy work in the area.

The capital that backed this enormous industrial expansion came increasingly through the agency of big city banks, for while successful local enterprises often started on the shoe-string financing available from investors in the immediate vicinity, and profits ploughed back in sufficed for a time to extend operations, eventually company directors tended to seek additional capital from new stock or bond issues, and these ordinarily required the services of investment banking houses. The lengthening list of stocks offered the public after the mid-1890s testified to the growing importance of this form of financing. Indeed, after the National Banking Act of 1863 had undermined shaky state banks and encouraged the concentration of monetary reserves in a few central institutions with national charters, New York bankers, first and foremost, with Philadelphia's and Boston's close seconds, became the principal underwriters of American industrial developments, although banking and investment houses in Chicago, St Louis, and San Francisco, to name only the most powerful of the regional centres, performed a similar service within narrower geographical limits. The financial role of these cities rested largely upon the power exercised through their security and commodity exchanges; the rise of trusts enlarged it.

The New York Stock Exchange, founded in 1817, was the oldest, and, thanks at least partly to its instituting loans callable on demand, the most firmly established, but every major city in the Union opened a local exchange before 1865. 'Wall Street', wrote a visitor to San Francisco in 1869, 'can teach Montgomery Street nothing...' Pacific coast financiers displayed 'a boldness, a sagacity, a vim, that can hardly be matched anywhere in the world.' To Chicago the 'Pit' was probably of even greater importance than her securities exchange. 'Corners' on, say, wheat made fortunes overnight and, perhaps because of a sudden shift in the weather, destroyed them as quickly. Neither ups nor downs, however, lessened the fearful respect that the Pit and Chicago's grain elevators inspired in farmers of the Illinois and Iowa corn country and of the wheat belt stretching from southern Kansas to central Minnesota. The Pit held even Minneapolis millers in semi-vassalage. And long before the boll weevil added a new uncertainty to bidding on cotton futures on the Memphis Cotton Exchange, Memphis's business standing rose in proportion to the size and number of transactions conducted by her cotton brokerage firms.

'Combinations in restraint of trade', such as the Standard Oil Company, the American Sugar Refining Company, and the United States Steel Corporation, fortified the financial overlordship of a few urban baronies, if only because of the overlapping membership on the boards of directors of metropolitan banks and the great corporations. For investment banks like the House of Morgan generally arranged the mergers that created the trusts and, as part of the bargain, held places on the directorates. As over 1,850 mergers between 1895 and 1902 established new industrial giants, Wall Street, Milk Street in Boston, Philadelphia's Market Street, Chicago's LaSalle Street, and Montgomery Street on the West Coast controlled much of the economy. Antitrust legislation failed to reverse the trend towards concentration.

With the perfecting of the internal combustion engine about 1901, a new element, however, entered into the complex of factors affecting urban growth. For the automobile not only promised Americans greater mobility than either steamboats or railroads provided, but transformed Detroit, Michigan, into the giant of an industry of unpredictable potentialities. Whether the upshot would be a diffusion of urban power or a heightened centripetalism was not at first certain. In fact why automobile-making early gravitated towards Detroit is still a moot question. In 1900 the port of the river that connects the upper with the lower Great Lakes was only one of a dozen places where small shops had been experimenting with developing horseless carriages; by 1910 the city could call herself the 'motor centre of the world'. Perhaps the reason lay in the skills of the considerable body of mechanics who for a generation had been building and repairing marine engines for ore boats and lake steamers.

Adopting the techniques of precision manufacture long familiar in making the interchangeable parts for firearms, clocks, sewing machines, and typewriters, the talented Ransom Olds and Henry Leland, taught by his experience at a government armoury during the Civil War, first introduced assembly lines into their automobile factories. Their plants gave new meaning to the term 'mass production'. Yet it was Henry Ford's decision in 1906 to abandon making high-priced cars and to produce a single, soundly engineered, inexpensive model to be sold only for cash that revolutionised the industry. Within two years the Ford Motor Company was turning out nearly a thousand Model 'T's' a month and grossing $6 million a year. Trucks and passenger cars in 1910 were not yet challenging the railroads, but even then the orders pouring out from Detroit's twenty automobile factories for steel, machine tools, rubber tyres, windshield glass, electric headlights, and lubricating oils were quickening industry in scores of cities, and, ultimately more significant, Ford's 'Tin Lizzie', priced within the purse of people of very modest means, was already lessening the isolation of farm families and hastening the movement of city families into the residential suburbs that had cropped up in the 1890s in the wake of electric trolley lines.

Of the social changes attending this half-century of industrial expansion, the most striking was the sharpened disparity of wealth between class and class in the cities. Pronounced differences in economic status had existed from the mid-seventeenth century onwards, but the rise in the last quarter of the nineteenth century of great fortunes controlled by fewer than a half-hundred families created a plutocracy that bore little resemblance to anything Americans had known before. Neither cultivated taste nor long-established social prestige mattered much in the new social order. Power, and with it social standing, now rested solely upon money, money acquired more often than not by pre-emption of water, oil, mineral, and timber rights in the public domain, by manipulation of securities on the stock exchanges, or by exploitation of industrial wage-earners. While the achievements of the 'robber barons' inevitably evoked admiration and envy, their unscrupulousness also awakened indignation. The careers of such men as the obscure Cleveland clerk, John D. Rockefeller, who in creating the Standard Oil Company made himself a multimillionaire, or of the railroad magnate, William K. Vanderbilt, whose comment 'the public be damned' summarised the point of view common among his associates and competitors, or of Andrew Carnegie, an eleven-year-old Scottish immigrant boy when he landed in Pittsburgh, who worked his way up in the tough world of the steel mills to found his own company and later organise the steel trust—all had a compelling fascination. Yet under the heavy tread of these and men like them the old American dream of equality crumbled. And inasmuch as the builders of the great fortunes were invariably urbanites at the heights of their careers, in the cities the vivid contrast between their mode of life and that of other citizens was ever-present.

As the work force at industrial plants rose into the thousands, the intimate relations that, despite some absentee ownership, had existed between management and employees in the mills and factories of the 1850s vanished. Machine-shop operators, steel workers, and textile mill hands all too often became labour, a commodity to be handled like raw materials, bought as cheaply as the supply permitted and replaced when the purchase price threatened to cut in upon profits. And the ever-renewing throng of European immigrants guaranteed replacements. As a consequence, factory workers found themselves caught in a situation which a move to another industrial plant or another city would merely worsen. Business executives, professional men, shopkeepers, salesmen, and people willing to turn farmers might still shift from one locale to another; industrial wage-earners in the last decades of the century generally stayed put.

The changing character of immigration added another new factor in the 1880s. When immigrants from eastern and southern Europe began to crowd into the receiving station set up on Ellis Island in New York harbour, language barriers cut off foreign-born workers from native-born. Some of the invaders succeeded in opening small shops or sold wares from pushcarts in the streets of the new colonies springing up, nationality by nationality, in the big northern cities; but non-English-speaking newcomers also swelled the industrial labour force. The German, Irish, and French Canadian Catholics who had come a generation earlier resented the intruders irrespective of their religion. Among American-born under-dogs sheer economics was probably the main force in reviving the anti-foreign, anti-Catholic sentiment that had run strong in mid-century. Curiously enough, now, forty years later, it was middle-class Americans without factories to man who sponsored the new American Protective Association and its fight against Catholicism. Intent upon keeping America for Anglo-Saxon Protestant Americans, they disliked and feared the aliens whose alien quality was emphasised by strange languages—Italian, Polish, Lithuanian, Yiddish, Czech, Hungarian, Russian, and Greek. Whether Roman Catholic, Greek Orthodox, Jewish, or, even worse, atheists, the new arrivals seemed to constitute an unassimilable, obscurely frightening proletarian mass.

The outbreak of fiercely fought strikes nourished the apprehensions of city dwellers engaged in the professions and in occupations only remotely linked to industry. Beginning with a countrywide railway workers' strike in 1877, progressing to Chicago's Haymarket Riot in 1886 when a bomb thrown at police dispersing protesting strikers from the McCormick Reaper works killed a policeman and spread hysteria through the city, and culminating in pitched battles in the early 1890s between industrial workers and the police or strike-breakers hired by employers, anarchy seemed to the timid and frightened onlooker to be engulfing American urban civilisation. Many an ordinarily sober citizen persuaded himself that this must be the work of foreign-born agitators blind to the blessings offered in this land of the free. Yet common sense eventually reminded him that for numberless working men those blessings consisted chiefly of meagre wages, long hours, grim working conditions, and no compensation for injuries incurred on the job. City newspapers generally thundered denunciations at strikers while the battles were in progress, but usually admitted later that all right did not lie on the side of employers. Furthermore, as the trade unions that banded together into the American Federation of Labor in 1886 enrolled as many native-born as immigrant members, the illusion that labour-capital conflicts were a purely foreign importation gradually dissipated. Although the building trades, the cigar-makers, the garment workers and other AFL unions rarely met with success when striking for better pay and shorter hours, citizens in every walk of life were slowly forced to recognise the labour movement as a permanent element in the industrialising nation.

The recurrent violence in the industrial communities—and, with the exception of the capital at Washington, by the early 1890s virtually every city of any importance contained factories—deepened the countryman's distrust of the city. When an attempted political alliance of disgruntled farmers and city workmen brought the Populist party into being, its leaders counted on common grievances against the 'money power' to sustain the Populist Revolt. It fell apart mainly because rural America nursed doubts about urban goals, and urban labour felt no kinship with the tenant farmers of the South or independent farmers elsewhere whose independence was

D

threatened by crop failures, extortionate railroad freight charges, and impending mortgage foreclosures. In the Deep South, demagogues succeeded only in fanning a racism that permitted whites to justify the lynching of Negroes. Four years of world-wide depression beginning in 1893, coupled with the 'closing' of the American frontier when word spread that claimants had taken up all good arable land in the United States, did little to narow the gulf between city and country. Still, between 1880 and 1910 at least 11 million Americans born in rural homes became urbanites, over a tenth again as many as the foreign arrivals of those years. Meanwhile if the swelling volume of immigration, in 1907 alone totalling more than 1·25 million souls, troubled most native-born families, they were not yet wholly ready to repudiate the inscription carved in 1903 on the base of the Statue of Liberty inviting the Old World to 'Give me your tired, your poor, your huddled masses yearning to be free'.

The renewing confidence of the urban middle classes probably kept anti-foreign sentiment within bounds. For steadily mounting industrial might, particularly after the business recovery at the end of the century, benefited them as well as the 'captains of industry'. As corporations replaced partnerships and family-owned firms run by fathers, sons, and sons-in-law, obscure young men with some education but without personal connections to recommend them were able to find places in the business hierarchy and work up to responsible managerial posts. At the same time, the nearly universal use of the typewriter and telephone in offices that had formerly relied upon letterpress copies of handwritten correspondence increased the number of jobs open to women who until then had had a precarious foothold in the business world. Growing emphasis on mechanisation in every phase of industrial production heightened the importance of institutes of technology and inspired boys to study engineering in preparation for careers in that rapidly expanding profession. Frequently financed by powerful industrialists, the schools of technology added a new field to higher education and endowed its professors with a special prestige. Advertising firms undertaking to enlarge factory sales needed commercial artists and writers capable of turning out catchy slogans; and magazines and trade journals supported by advertising were eager to enlist talent.

Well before a constitutional amendment of 1913 sanctioned a graduated federal income tax, corporation record-keeping reached a complexity that called for high-salaried certified public accountants. In this fashion new occupations obliterated fears that the nation had slipped into the hands of a small all-powerful plutocracy. People neither rich nor individually very important came to realise that they, members of the urban middle class, still formed the backbone of American society. The great machines of industry and the networks of commerce could not operate without them.

5

SOCIAL AND POLITICAL ADJUSTMENTS

1860–1910

Conflict and confusion in everyday life were inescapable facets of the response to industrialism. That the people of the United States succeeded in adjusting at all to such far-reaching change was due in some measure to the public schools. Whatever their faults, and they were many, the common schools gave city children some common background and induced in parents awareness of the common needs and aims that, John Dewey said, tie society together. True, the 'melting pot' did not melt well enough to fully assimilate the 17 million foreign-born who came during the half-century. True, also, that Protestant-Catholic hostility endured; the opening of city parochial schools lessened but did not eradicate the feuding, since some citizens saw dangers in thus cutting off Catholic children from wholesome contacts with the non-Catholic majority. Equally true, Southern cities, where private and charity institutions had done duty in antebellum days, first inaugurated public schools in the Recon-struction era, and then only for children in the elementary and grammar grades. Under an educational system of racial segregation, tax-supported Negro schools were generally badly equipped, taught by ill-trained teachers, and rarely offered more than five years of instruction. Even in the national capital, where Northerners in Congress dictated the establishment of coloured public schools in the last year of the Civil War, Negro children for four generations attended segregated schools labelled 'separate but equal', but manifestly far from equal.

Public education throughout the country had suffered during and immediately after the Civil War, but Northern and Western cities, confronted with expanding populations of school age, soon set about enlarging facilities, and in the 1880s they began revamping methods of instruction. School superintendents and teachers in a dozen places scattered from Boston to St Louis began to try out new pedagogical ideas, above all stressing techniques calculated to improve pupils' understanding rather than emphasising rote learning. While the reports of William Harris, who had had long experience in St Louis before he became United States Commissioner of Education, called attention to innovations, the demonstrations John Dewey and Francis Parker conducted in Chicago and William Bramwell Powell carried out in Washington showed the value of relaxing rigid discipline and encouraging children to 'learn by doing'. The heightened interest children displayed in their studies helped win acceptance for the new educational approach. Simultaneously schooling began to reach downward to include kindergartens and upward to add four years of high school. By 1886 nearly four hundred cities had opened high schools, and by 1900 over a million young children were enjoying kindergarten classes. State universities further extended the range of free education. After 1904, as the General Education Board, one of John D. Rockefeller's philanthropies, taught Southern communities what good schools could mean and how to finance them, cities in the Deep South began to establish high schools and to devote increasing attention to public education at every level.

In the big centres of population, moreover, the urgent need to keep children off the streets and to teach immigrant children about their new country led to the appointment of truant officers. Their efforts seldom kept attendance at more than about 60 per cent of the pupils enrolled, partly because few states had enacted child labour laws. The common schools nevertheless 'Americanised' several million immigrant children while giving them a rudimentary general education. Furthermore, the desire of big industrial and commercial concerns to obtain technically trained workers encouraged several cities to follow Baltimore's example of 1883, in opening manual training schools at the secondary level. Before 1905 thirty-four cities were maintaining public trade or factory schools, and night schools where young people and adults could learn English were helping the foreign-born to adapt themselves to American ways. Adult Americanisation classes not only prepared aliens for naturalisation but in the process raised the urban literacy rate. Urban literacy, indeed, was consistently higher than rural.

Unhappily, neither public education nor any other public service escaped the consequences of corrupt and incompetent municipal government. Special taxes earmarked for school support supposedly freed boards of education from politicians' interference, but even so school administration often became a political football. Superintendents who had angled for appointment might pay their political debts by giving their backers profitable contracts for new buildings and supplies or by finding teaching posts for their protégés. Inefficiency, if not outright dishonesty, ran costs up and left school systems burdened with debt. State subsidies might come to the rescue, but legislatures in rural states tended to be wary of city institutions. Once graft penetrated the city hall, taxpayers paid an increasingly heavy price for fire and police protection, health supervision, street paving, extension of water and sewage systems, regulation of street railways and poor relief, and the services were of an inferior order.

'The government of cities', the British scholar James A. Bryce wrote in 1888, 'is the one conspicuous failure of the United States.' New York was the first to fall into the clutches of a skilfully organised political machine. When William Tweed, the most notorious of the city bosses, became Grand Sachem of Tammany Hall in 1868, he had behind him some eighteen years of experience in aligning ward heelers to round up votes and party contributions and in pushing through metropolitan bills that netted him and his henchmen ample rewards. He milked the city treasury of more than $200 million before reformers succeeded in exposing him, bringing him to trial, and eventually sending him to prison. But New York was not alone. *The Shame of the Cities*, as Lincoln Steffens entitled the collection of articles he prepared in 1902 and 1903 for a popular magazine, covered a half-dozen other municipalities and might have included more: Philadelphia, 'corrupt and contented'; Pittsburgh; Cincinnati; Chicago; St Louis, where greedy industrialists took control; Minneapolis, ruled by a crook, a venal police force, and degenerates at the bottom of the social pyramid; San Francisco, run by a labour demagogue who battened on the profits of organised vice and the 'slush funds' paid in by utility companies; New Orleans, held captive by race prejudice and her local Tammany, the Choctaws. There were exceptions. Mayor Hazen Pingree gave Detroit an honest administration in the 1890s and, when elected state governor in 1896, carried on the fight. 'Golden Rule' Jones, Mayor of Toledo from 1897 till his death in 1904, put the city police on Civil Service, introduced an eight-hour day and a minimum wage for all city employees, and inaugurated free concerts and kindergartens. Cleveland had an enviable record under the vigorous and enlightened Tom Johnson, famous throughout the country for his successful 'penny carfare' campaign. Seattle's government also was relatively clean. Otherwise, few cities altogether avoided the contamination of graft.

Corruption in municipal government had sprung up like a toadstool wherever community leadership faltered. During the unsettled years immediately following the war, individual and corporate entrepreneurs, lawyers, and doctors, preoccupied with their private affairs and, if politically ambitious, interested only in careers in the state or national arena, preferred to leave the increasingly onerous chores of local administration to anyone willing to undertake them. So incompetents and scalawags moved into public office. If accumulating civic needs brought about appeals to state legislatures for special commissions to handle such problems as building and managing city waterworks or taking charge of police departments, the usual result was a division of authority, the resignation of honest officials, and a breakdown in civic morale that strengthened boss rule. Once bosses were in the saddle they cracked the whip over underlings. Police departments were peculiarly vulnerable to political pressures. In 1865 only the seven largest cities in the country and the national capital had uniformed salaried police forces; within a decade unemployment pushed crime rates upward till most municipalities felt obliged to adopt the system. Sheriffs' posses chasing horse thieves across the Western plains had an easier life than conscientious city patrolmen. Usually recruited by ward politicians, generally ill-trained, and always badly underpaid, policemen as a rule were less servants of the public than creatures of the local political machine, giving protection to its friends and to illegal interests ready to pay for the privilege.

Bosses' financial support came chiefly from the *quid pro quo* paid over by traction and gas companies for franchises and from the underworld of gamblers, prostitutes, and operators of the unlicensed liquor establishments known as 'blind pigs'. Political support, on the other hand, rested quite as much upon the gratitude slum dwellers and voters a few economic notches above them felt towards the men who gave their wants some consideration. For most city bosses, however intent on lining their own pockets, were warm-hearted, loyal to their friends, and glad to help humble people of the class from which they themselves sprang. At least half the powerful machine politicians were Irish Catholics who had grown up in the cities from whose rich and well-born they now exacted toll. The rank and file of citizens were slow to see that boss rule with its perversion of power hurt the entire community, that it made a mockery of the fundamental concept of a 'government of laws, not men'. To 'throw the rascals out' proved to be a gargantuan task even after their victims realised what was at stake. Full realisation generally came only after flagrant abuses destroyed public indifference and complacency.

Sooner or later reformers made some headway against corruption. Public-spirited newspaper editors and Thomas Nast's cartoons aroused New Yorkers in the 1870s to drive out Boss Tweed. But several of his successors in Tammany had highly dubious records, and reform administrations rarely lasted more than a term or two. At the opening of the new century 'muckrakers' like Lincoln Steffens were still struggling to stir city electorates to rebellion. The Reform Club of New York, Committees of 100 in a number of cities, Philadelphia's Municipal League, Chicago's Municipal Voters' League, the American Civic Association, and the body to which Henry Leland in Detroit gave an evangelical caste by calling it The Civic Uplift League all helped the cause. The Conferences for Good City Government, begun in 1895, perhaps helped even more by providing a nation-wide forum. Earnest people everywhere talked about encouraging citizen participation in local government, 'getting out the vote', and nurturing the democratic process. But churchmen determined to combat vice, supporters of the Anti-Saloon League and the Women's Christian Temperance Union campaigning against the demon rum, educators aiming at better public schools, and businessmen anxious to cut taxes and to recapture and centralise local control did not always see eye to eye about primary objectives or methods. In Pittsburgh, for example, young business executives led a successful fight for a new charter that reduced the city council to nine aldermen, all elected at large, but while the charter proponents manifestly wanted efficiency, they also wanted fewer neighbourhood groups with ward aldermen representing ward interests, a weaker, not a stronger, voice from foreign-born citizens—in short, less, not more, democracy. And yet Pittsburghers started *The Survey*, a journal that presented the most penetrating and thorough analysis of urban problems that appeared in the United States before 1915.

Naturalised immigrants usually took the party label of the local political boss who befriended them, but if they voted in national elections, as part of the urban labour force they tended to join with native American working men in supporting the party that stood for high protective tariffs. Yet New York with a stongly entrenched Tammany, Boston, and San Francisco were Democratic party strongholds in the 1880s, the decade of heaviest immigration of any ten-year period in the century. The depression of the 1890s, on the other hand, swung them into the Republican fold. Although muckrakers were prone to call the Republican party of that era a close ally of the Standard Oil Trust and big business, industrial workers in northern cities generally looked upon it as the party of prosperity and progress. Southern cities, on the contrary, from reconstruction days on clung to the Democratic party, the opponent of carpetbaggers and 'niggers'. And as one Southern state after another followed Louisiana's and Mississippi's example in disenfranchising coloured men, party alignment in the 'solid South'

D*

remained unaffected by any discontent among white working men in her growing textile towns and industrial cities. Elsewhere reformers in the early years of the twentieth century were beginning to advocate non-partisanship in city elections inasmuch as local issues were likely to have little connection with national party programmes, and yet good men, if unacceptable to party politicians at the state or national capitals, went down in defeat. The proposal gained relatively few adherents. The national and state party organisations were too useful to a majority of city office seekers for them to discard such assistance willingly.

Graft, incompetence, and misdirected zeal notwithstanding, urban services expanded year by year. Paved streets stretched out to the city's periphery, their surfaces frequently torn up to lay new gas, water, and sewer lines. Private companies usually supplied the gas, but most municipalities had to build or enlarge their own water works, sometimes at staggering cost. As soon as piped water became available to all city residents, the problem of sewage disposal began. Baltimore had some 90,000 backyard privies as late as 1900, and Washington still had several thousand in the 1930s, but in Northern cities insistence upon less primitive arrangements hastened the introduction of plumbing during the 1880s. When epidemiologists in Boston and boards of health elsewhere proved the connection between contaminated water and the incidence of typhoid and dysentery, taxpayers also accepted the necessity of paying for underground trunk lines to carry sewage beyond the city limits out into bays or rivers where sunlight would purify it. Attempts to stop the sale of adulterated milk were less successful until city boards of health got backing from several state legislatures in the 1890s and thenceforward were able to conduct moderately effective inspections of dairy herds. Safeguards for public health went still further when some 400 cities, following the example set by Boston, Chicago, and New York, instituted regular medical inspections in the public schools.

Transportation for the ever-growing throngs called for street railways in the 1870s in all but the smallest communities. While the failure of New York's horse-car service to keep pace with population pushed tenements higher and packed their occupants tighter and tighter, other cities managed to spread out fast enough to avoid comparable congestion. When electric-powered trolleys became feasible in 1887, traction 'moguls' began to buy up the franchises of city horse-car lines, effected consolidations, formed holding companies, and then bribed city councils into granting them new long-term franchises, some of them good for fifty years—in the case of Pittsburgh and several other boss-ridden cities, for 999 years. In New York and Chicago elevated tracks raised on steel girders to some thirty feet above street level supplemented trolleys but darkened the streets. At least the 'Els' lessened the hazards of pedestrians subject to the whims of trolley motormen. In Brooklyn the cars zoomed along at such reckless speed that the city's baseball team was nicknamed the 'Trolley Dodgers'. Although the traction monopolies exploited the public unmercifully, the lengthening lines permitted a dispersion of population important to every mushrooming city. Inter-urban trolley lines carried that dispersion into suburban areas also. Around Boston 'street-car suburbs' reached astonishing proportions before the close of the century. Boston, whose narrow streets of the business district still followed the course of the seventeenth-century cowpaths to the Common, was the first American city to open a subway. Seven years later, in 1904, New York completed part of a more elaborate Underground and by 1910 had a hundred miles in use. Philadelphia built a relatively short subway in the heart of the city about the same time.

Despite improving transit, rising land values and population growth combined to create slums in more cities than New York. By the 1880s in Boston, Brooklyn, Newark, and Chicago, teeming three- and four-storey tenements crammed two and three families into every living unit. In Philadelphia and Baltimore the pattern varied only in the height of the tight-packed rows of houses. Tucked out of sight from the streets, in Washington, alley-dwellings overflowing with Negro families shared sunless inner courts with commodious stables for horses. A decade after publication of the report of 1857 on conditions in New York, a Tenement House law attempted to impose limits on the number of people a building could accommodate, and in 1887 further regulation required inside plumbing and fire escapes. Both laws proved unenforceable; in 1890 some 30,000 tenement buildings in Manhattan contained over a million people. The building codes adopted in other big cities were equally ineffective. A third housing law enacted for New York in 1901 was more skilfully written, had sharper teeth, and won wider public support than the earlier acts, but as long as newcomers had to choose between squalid quarters or none at all, city slums spread and the menace to public health widened.

Housing investigations conducted in several cities and a Congressional inquiry of 1892 went far towards awakening Americans to the wretchedness about them. If the city dweller who had grown up in the United States in the ebullient era of Manifest Destiny was at first incredulous that abject poverty could have reached such proportions in a single generation, study of the reports or newspaper and magazine comments dispelled his doubts. While some people shrugged their shoulders, a wave of humanitarianism, civic pride, and a sense of social guilt swept others into a search for means of alleviating and ultimately eradicating these ills. At the end of the 1880s three young Americans visited Toynbee Hall in London and returned to open a neighbourhood Guild and the College Settlement in New York's slums. Bostonians, Chicagoans, and Philadelphians followed that example.

When Jane Addams founded Hull House in an industrial section of Chicago where factories and warehouses stood interspersed among brick tenements, frame shacks, and once roomy private houses converted into warrens of two-room 'apartments', she was troubled not only by the material want of her neighbours in this immigrant quarter, but also by the oppressive sense of isolation that enveloped the older people among them. Peasants transplanted from Polish or Bohemian or Greek villages to this English-speaking industrial world of a big American city were unable to connect the present with their past. The German musician now scrubbing floors in a Chicago office building and the Italian goldsmith shovelling coal in a factory were similarly bewildered. Their lack of power 'to see life as a whole', wrote Miss Addams, 'is the most fruitful source of misunderstandings between European immigrants and their children, as it is between them and their American neighbours'. At the same time many of the children came to grief 'through their premature fling into city life, having thrown off parental control as they have impatiently discarded foreign ways'. Equally painful to observe was the treatment the children of other people accorded the most foreign-looking of the elderly immigrants—'the Italians whose fruit carts are upset simply because they are "dagoes", or the Russian peddlers who are stoned . . . because it has become a code of honour in a gang of boys to thus express their derision'. The prejudices that underlay such behaviour, Miss Addams added, 'would be much minimised in America, if we faced our own race problem with courage and intelligence'. Although poverty stemming from peri- odic unemployment, low wages, and illness was not confined to the foreign-born, its native American victims, white or coloured, rarely lived in the immigrant section of city slums; the alien after all was alien.

When the depression of the nineties ran unemployment up to an estimated 50,000 in each of the country's three largest cities and to a total of more than 800,000 in fifty other municipalities, settlement houses sprang up in a half-hundred other places. Some were non- sectarian in origin, others were sponsored by Episcopal, Jewish, and Presbyterian congregations, and in 1895 Cincinnati Catholics estab- lished the first Catholic settlement. While the genuine warmth emanating from these volunteer institutions produced a true sense of community with revitalising effects in depressed urban neigh- bourhoods, participants quickly realised that private charity was not enough. Charity Organisation Societies modelled on those of London and Berlin had emerged in the early 1880s, to be succeeded by Associated Charities designed to prevent duplication of effort among the scores of secular and church philanthropies, but the relief measures possible under a system of private endeavour, no matter how earnest or how efficiently organised, could not handle the problems arising in periods of economic distress.

Public institutions to care for indigents, the ill, the widows and orphans, the aged and the insane never had money enough during boom times, and when hard times set in and the burden increased, city welfare budgets lagged still further behind the amounts needed. In boss-ridden cities politics tended to determine who received out- door relief. Moreover, two generally accepted concepts hampered

the development of public welfare programmes. First was the
enduring idea that the provisions of the Elizabethan poor laws as
adopted in the colonial period marked out reasonable limits for
public action; individual charity must undertake anything more
extensive. Second was the fear of encouraging pauperism, a fear
enhanced by Herbert Spencer's writings on social Darwinism and
the folly of fostering the survival of the humanly unfit; Spencer's
essays long enjoyed wide popularity in the United States. Both
concepts underwent re-examination before the end of the 1890s.
Although endorsements of the principle of public responsibility for
the well-being of all citizens had to wait for the 1930s, city dwellers'
campaigns for larger public support for the needy bore some fruit
at the turn of the century. As Boards of Charities to supervise the
spending of tax money came into being, detailed reports on their
activities called attention to persistent wants. Public hospitals multiplied, and child-care agencies staffed by trained public servants
gradually persuaded their communities of the advantages of foster
homes over orphanages for their charges.

   In nurturing an awareness of urban needs and ways of meeting
them the spread of the Social Gospel played a major part. While
the deep religious convictions that had animated antebellum communities gave way to a new secularism, the effectiveness of Jewish
and Catholic bodies in organising charity for their own people
spurred Protestants on to direct their energies outward instead of
inward at the state of their souls. Washington Gladden, a Congregational minister whose pastorates in two Massachusetts industrial
cities and later in Columbus, Ohio, exposed him to a first-hand
view of the conditions among the working classes, was the first
apostle of the movement to obtain a wide hearing. In the recurrent
strikes and periods of depression his ability to sympathise with and
weigh the rights and wrongs of both workers and employers
made him a welcome mediator in labour disputes and enabled him
to show the utility of labour-management conferences. His article
entitled 'The Cosmopolitan City Club' outlining the steps by which
citizens could share in ameliorating distress inspired the formation of
civic associations and city clubs in a number of places. Though the
best known of the advocates of a religion aimed at social betterment

he was not alone in persuading Christians that the future of the church in urban America rested upon service to the labouring classes. Walter Rauschenbusch, Baptist organiser of the Brotherhood of the Kingdom and author of *Christianity and the Social Crisis*, William S. Rainsford, rector of St George's in New York, where he introduced his parishioners to church work in the form of running a community centre, Graham Taylor, a professor at the Chicago Theological Seminary who took his students into the Chicago slums to see for themselves, and other ministers contributed to making the 'institutional church' a constructive force in city life.

In 1906 a congressman from a Michigan farming district won brief notoriety in the United States capital by blasting a proposal to spend public money for playgrounds and playground directors in Washington. 'God,' he pontificated, 'taught children to play.' Forty years earlier few Americans would have quarrelled with him. Even Manhattan at that time had some vacant lots where boys could play ball. Newer cities were still less compactly built; an hour's walk would take one beyond the straggling outskirts into open country. By 1890 the countryside had receded to the distant horizon, and in metropolitan centres children of the poorer areas had only the city streets to play in. School yards were closed after school hours, and city parks, where they existed at all, were primarily reserved for sedate adults. So, under the prodding of settlement house leaders and church groups who had begun to open playgrounds, city councils acquired sites, equipped them with sand boxes, swings, horizontal bars, and wading and swimming pools, and engaged supervisors to take charge of games. Converts organised the Playground Association of America while the Michigan congressman was inveighing against such socialistic folly. Eighty cities were maintaining public playgrounds by 1910, and forty had zoos.

Adult outdoor recreation ran towards organised sport, especially after city baseball teams formed a National League and in 1901 a second, the American League, to contend for the world's championship. With rich and poor flocking to the ball parks to cheer their nines, baseball became a social cement between class and class. Bicycling, boating, tennis, and golf, though long too expensive to lie within everyone's reach, had a wide vogue, widened further once municipalities discovered the feasibility of opening public facilities and renting equipment to impecunious patrons. While race tracks on city outskirts drew gamblers from every social level, on the city streets fine carriages drawn by thoroughbreds marked their owners as part of the urban élite until expensive automobiles began to replace horseflesh; when Model-T Fords pre-empted space on the public ways, the horse and buggy rapidly became an anachronism. Meanwhile, summer resorts in hot weather emptied the cities of hundreds of families. Two weeks' holiday or less in a cottage on a nearby lake might be the limit for a shopkeeper or a bank clerk, but many middle-class householders contrived longer vacations in the mountains or at the seaside. San Franciscans took themselves up into the Sierras. People to the eastward travelled for miles to camp in the high mountains of Estes Park above Denver. From the blistering heat of the corn belt the exodus was to the woods of northern Michigan and Wisconsin. Newport, after a century of oblivion, became a favourite haunt of the very rich, with Bar Harbour on Mt Desert in Maine a competitor from the 1890s onwards.

The winter season brought crowds to city theatres, dance halls, and opera houses. Indeed plays in New York often ran the year round. Although Broadway dominated the American theatre world after 1870, popular plays, musicals, melodrama, vaudeville, and burlesque shows drew enthusiastic audiences in every city with any pretensions to culture. Opera performances were rarer, but Denver, where mining kings spent much of their time, acquired a magnificent opera house in 1881, and eight years later the newly built Chicago Auditorium, with a larger seating capacity than New York's 'Met', was packed nightly. After 1900, cinema houses introduced novel entertainment. Initially suspect as subversive of morality, movies quickly overcame prejudice except among strict Methodists and hard-shell Baptists. While pianos found their way into private homes and bar-rooms in the remotest parts of the country, jazz, born in New Orleans' waterfront dives, crept north to St Louis and Chicago and spread thence, despite orthodox musicians' disdain of its beating rhythm and haunting undertones. With

Negro bands playing 'blues' in night clubs of the city Gold Coasts, 'dance mad' young people added the fox-trot to their repertories of waltz and two-step. In the meantime city orchestras and classical music gained fresh support. The struggle to sustain full symphonic orchestras sometimes collapsed, but, abetted by the multiplying musical conservatories, they survived in the metropolitan centres. By the early years of the new century sophisticated European conductors remarked upon the accomplished performances to be heard in the 'Land of the Dollar'. Manifestly America's urban jungle nurtured some forms of artistry.

Yet among novelists angry criticism of the barbarities of the city became an increasingly common theme. After exploding his protests in *The Gilded Age*, Mark Twain turned for escape to the small mid-western town setting of Tom Sawyer and Huck Finn. As early as 1871 Walt Whitman, who had once felt the pull of New York, wrote of 'cities, crowded with petty grotesques, malformations, phantoms, playing meaningless antics'. Jack London's savage attacks conveyed none of the romantic aura of Bret Harte's tales of the Far West. Surveying the scene from Boston, William Dean Howells adopted a milder tone, but his distaste for what lay about him shone through in novels reviewers called 'Boston-Torn-to-Tatters'. Theodore Dreiser's *Sister Carrie* portrayed Chicago's vitality in the 1880s, but his later books delineated Manhattan's cruel impersonality, while Henry James, an expatriate in London, spoke of New York's 'appalling greed' and dismissed her skyscraper skyline as a 'pincushion in profile'. After describing San Francisco's fascinations and demoralising influences in *McTeague*, Frank Norris went on to excoriate in *The Octopus* the brutalising commercialism of all city life. Upton Sinclair's *The Jungle* lashed out furiously at the exploitation of Chicago's stockyard workers and at the degradation of the city about them. Although 'Mr Dooley', the witty Irish pubkeeper whom Peter Finley Dunne created as his mouthpiece, seasoned his commentaries with a humour that lessened their sting, the sting was there.

From Thomas Jefferson onwards American intellectuals had objected to the city as an unwholesome entity; with the rise of the teeming industrial city of the 1880s and after, their protests acquired new force. At Harvard the philosopher Josiah Royce pointed to the disruptiveness stemming from the excessive mobility of unassimilated strangers in urban America. Fearful of the mob spirit, he deplored the effects of the massive forces that crushed the individual in the city, where 'we tend . . . to read the same daily news, to share the same general ideas . . . to live in the same external fashions . . . and to approach a dead level of harassed mediocrity'. John Dewey, William James, and subscribers to their pragmatic philosophy, on the other hand, were less troubled by the prospect of conformity than over the loss of common purpose, but they believed the city capable of developing a saving community spirit. Like James, Dewey disliked bigness, but the common school, he contended, could 'be made a genuine form of community life'. He would elaborate his concept of the Great Community in the 1920s.

Unlike novelists, American painters rarely depicted the harsh aspects of the urban scene. George Innes painted only country landscapes, John La Farge religious subjects, Winslow Homer canvases of the Adirondacks and seascapes, John Singer Sargent chiefly portraits. James McNeill Whistler, Mary Cassatt, and, until 1916, Joseph Pennell lived abroad. Thomas Eakins, whose distinguished work won him scant recognition during his lifetime, urged his pupils in Philadelphia 'to peer deeper into the heart of American life', but in so far as that heart lay in the big cities his plea had no effect until the 'Ash Can' school began to emerge about 1905. When that group, at least half of whom had begun their careers as newspaper draughtsmen and magazine illustrators, held a first show in 1908, a critic declared that Robert Henri, George Luks, and George Bellows 'deliberately and conscientiously paint the ugly wherever it occurs'. It occurred most often in the cities. But as dealers refused to handle the 'veritists'' work, exhibits in the public galleries still consisted chiefly of paintings or copies of the old masters, a few French impressionists, and Americans who dealt with orthodox subjects. To the viewing public, more important than subject matter was the growing number of museums where paintings and sculpture could be seen.

Native artistic originality showed most clearly in the urban architecture of the Chicago school of the last two decades of the nineteenth century. As William LeBaron Janney and his younger associates, notably Louis Sullivan, John Root, and John Holabird, changed the face of downtown Chicago, architects elsewhere adopted many of their basic ideas: skyscrapers resting solidly on columns going down to bed rock, superstructures of steel girders faced with light masonry walls banded horizontally with windows, and simplicity of line from top to bottom of the ten to twenty storeys. Janney's plans also called for leaving sections of every floor without permanent partitions so that tenants could subdivide the space to suit themselves. Designed for office buildings and big hotels in business districts where land values were high, the new style had little effect on domestic architecture. Still the turrets and bay windows of the Victorian age lost popularity in residential areas, and in the Midwest the stark horizontal planes of Frank Lloyd Wright's 'prairie houses' were awakening interest.

Leading New York firms, to be sure, never adopted or soon abandoned the functional simplicity that characterised the Chicago school. Thus Richard Morris Hunt clung to the classical style in building the new Metropolitan Museum of Art and reproduced sumptuous Italian palaces in the 'summer cottages', the 'Marble House' and 'The Breakers', he designed for William K. and Cornelius Vanderbilt at Newport. The Columbia University Library, the work of Charles McKim's firm, was a pantheon of steps, Ionic columns, and dome which left the reading room in semi-darkness. But the twenty-five-storey Flatiron Building on Times Square and the skyscrapers rising along lower Broadway made the Manhattan skyline by 1910 a sight the most knowledgeable globe-trotter could not forget.

A septuagenarian Rip Van Winkle returning to any American city in the early twentieth century could scarcely have credited his eyes. Not only had the haphazard, straggling appearance of ante-bellum days yielded to a densely built-up look, but here and there, amidst the brutal masses of stone and brick, parks and formal tree-lined boulevards pointed to a reaching for ordered beauty. Frederick Law Olmsted had laid out Central Park in New York City in the 1860s, and in the early 1870s landscaped the grounds of the Capitol in Washington, but, greatly admired though his work was, it had not made sufficient impression to persuade other cities to undertake formal programmes of beautification. City planning consequently received its initial impetus from the team of architects, sculptors, and landscapists, Olmsted among them, to whom Chicagoans entrusted the task of laying out the fair grounds for the Columbian Exposition of 1893. Local promoters who had adopted the slogan 'Make Culture Hum' were as overwhelmed as the country visitors to the fair at the beauty of the 'White City' that arose along the swampy lake shore to the south of Chicago. The achievement gave birth to the City Beautiful movement, for if a handful of artists could build in a year so exquisite a creation, eclectic though its architecture was, other men could emulate them, at least in formulating and adhering to a consistent overall scheme. The depression of the 1890s delayed action, but with returning prosperity cities from coast to coast set about drafting plans for land purchases and improvements that would enhance their looks.

Washington, where an advisory park commission mapped out an elaborate proposal, was the first city to see results. Congress authorised the removal of railroad tracks from the Mall and accepted the commission's recommendations about the location of new government buildings and the landscaping of the public domain. Elsewhere progress was largely on paper, although several cities launched campaigns to get rid of billboards and similar eyesores. While Boston laid out the park along the Fenway, she did little to develop the 5,000 acres of land beyond the city limits which she had bought in the 1890s for a public reacreation area; Chicago made no better headway in carrying out plans for a grand esplanade along her twenty-mile lake shore. San Francisco, nearly completely destroyed by an earthquake and fire in 1906, rejected a formal scheme for rebuilding. Yet ideas were germinating; in time Patrick Geddes' *City Development*, published in 1904, would bear some fruit. New Haven managed to restore some dignity to the old town green, and, in preparing for a centennial of the Louisiana Purchase, St Louis took a fresh look at the possibilities of her river front, the 'Gateway to the West'. Los Angeles planned a mile-long, two-hundred-foot-wide avenue ending in an impressive plaza.

Ridden with graft, vice, and crime, pocked with ugliness and human wretchedness, urban America was nevertheless stirring itself to build anew. Frederick C. Howe, a staunch supporter of 'Progressivism', in 1905 spelled out his optimism in *The City: The Hope of Democracy*, and it was more than sentimentality that led Katharine Lee Bates to insert in her hymn to 'America The Beautiful' the lines:

> O beautiful for patriot dream
> That sees beyond the years
> Thine alabaster cities gleam
> Undimmed by human tears.

6

THE SWING OF THE PENDULUM

The 'Progressive Era', as Americans labelled the first decade and a half of the twentieth century, ended with the Great Crusade 'to make the world safe for democracy'. Thereafter the national mood swung from one extreme to another, from idealistic optimism to cynical disillusionment, followed by an extravaganza of frivolity, the pursuit of applied science, and reliance on the solons of big business until the 'bust' of 1929, and then the despairs of all-enveloping depression. In the fat years the cities enjoyed greater prosperity than the farming countryside, and the upper classes an assurance not shared by city working men; in the very lean years everyone suffered. During the hardest times the European visitor was likely to be startled at the number of automobiles on American city streets and at hearing music and the wranglings of 'Amos 'n Andy' sound at night from radios in slum tenements. While farmers and villagers strove to check urban influences, and city dwellers themselves often sought to preserve the values of nineteenth-century agrarian America, the cinema, the automobile, and the radio were creating a country-wide conformity to city ideas and modes of behaviour. At the same time sheer numbers of people steadily reduced the role of the individual in metropolitan centres.

The nostalgia for a rural past expressed in much of the writing of the Progressive era blinded few observers of the United States in 1911 to the overriding importance of the city. Nor could intelligent people fail to note that cities no longer possessed the economic autonomy they had commanded in colonial times and for a century thereafter. Railroad networks and spreading industrial empires had brought 'geographic solar systems' into being within a national urban constellation. Wage rates varied somewhat from region to region, notably between the North and the Deep South, where the supply of poor-white labour was still abundant, and wherever inadequate transportation left pockets of local monopoly, commodity prices might run higher than elsewhere. But a national pattern prevailed in most of the economy, and the metropolitan suns set the orbital pattern. City bankers and investment houses, Wall Street's above all, still dominated the money market. Urban reformers intent on eradicating social ills look upon this concentration of economic power as the root of all evil; most of them believed any successful attack upon it would have to have national political support. The battlefield would be the city. Probably few Americans at that time realised that during the preceding fifty years the United States had been undergoing a revolution more profound than that of the 1770s.

Reform was in the air in 1911 and 1912. Like 'civil rights' a half-century later, the rallying cry in political campaigns was 'social justice'. The phrase carried various implications: to city working men it meant recognition of some form of collective bargaining; to owners of small businesses, curbs on the great trusts; to people engaged in the relatively new profession of social work, prohibition of child labour, regulation of sweat shops, and payment of mothers' pensions to help tide broken families over periods of crisis; to Negroes, chances for jobs which race prejudice denied them. Urban malaise weakened urban faith in the old-line Republican party, and when 'Teddy' Roosevelt broke with it to form the Bull Moose party the city vote split wide enough to put Woodrow Wilson, Democratic apostle of the 'New Freedom', into the White House.

National legislation in the next two years effected several significant social changes, not the least of which was the result of a graduated federal income tax that checked the pyramiding of great fortunes. But Congress left measures aimed at bettering the lot of city working people to the states and municipalities. In the industrial cities attempts of labour to organise effectively merely produced fresh suspicion among middle-class Americans and employers. Such progress as occurred in obtaining working men's compensation for injuries, limiting hours of work for women, granting mothers' pensions, and forbidding child labour came from legislatures of heavily industrialised states. Otherwise neither states nor municipalities accepted responsibility for enlarging public welfare services. Manifestly legislation alone was not going to transform 'the hope of democracy' into urban reality.

The most conspicuous failure of the New Freedom to establish equality lay in the realm of race relations. From West Coast cities diatribes still poured out against the 'Yellow Peril', despite a Gentleman's Agreement with Japan in 1908 which undercut the foundations of that type of nativism. In the South opposition to allowing the Negro either voting rights or a place in industry showed no signs of abating. On the contrary, while white paternalism towards Negroes who 'kept their place' preserved an outwardly peaceful atmosphere in many small towns, in the recently industrialised cities a new Ku Klux Klan, formed in 1915, found congenial soil, although its members, unlike those of the terrorist Klan of Reconstruction days, directed their attacks against Jews, Catholics, and foreigners, as well as Negroes. Oddly enough, Birmingham, Alabama, founded in 1871 and therefore lacking any antebellum paternalistic tradition to soften racial antagonisms, showed less intolerance than the textile towns that undertook to repress the 'uppity nigra' at every turn. In Washington, grown by 1913 to a city of a third of a million inhabitants, federal officials generally adopted a pattern of segregation for civil service employees, an arrangement that had begun a decade earlier but not spread far. Now its acceptance as official government policy immediately prompted private employers to limit coloured people to menial jobs. Negro aristocrats trained in the professions now became 'niggers'. The city known in the 1870s as 'the coloured man's paradise' reverted to the white supremacists. In the Northern cities trade unions continued to exclude Negroes from membership, and wherever coloured men attempted to join the ranks of industrial workers, hostility flared out, especially from second-generation naturalised Americans.

Except in the failure to breach the colour line, the drive for urban 'social betterment' nevertheless made some impression. Paving the way for other reforms, several communities substituted for mayors and councils three- to five-man boards of commissioners with or without single city managers to take charge of all municipal housekeeping. Instead of dividing responsibility among a score or more of city fathers who spent only part of their time on municipal affairs, the innovation concentrated authority in the hands of a small body who could be held to account. The plan grew out of a spreading belief that a city should be run like a business: if the executives proved inefficient they would not be re-elected and managers would be replaced at the expiration of their contracts. To the gratification of proponents of non-partisanship in municipal elections, the arrangement largely divorced city administration from national and state party politics. Wherever tried, the new schemes seemed to work well.

Among artists, strivings for a freer, more creative society found expression in 1913 in a show at the New York Armory where rebels exhibited their abstractions, and Marcel Duchamp's 'Nude Descending a Staircase' shocked the public. Although the selection sent to Chicago stirred the Law and Order League to campaign against its 'obscenities', the modernists believed they had scored a victory. 'Bustle and hopefulness', wrote the critic Malcolm Cowley, 'filled the early years, 1911–1916. . . . Everywhere new institutions were being founded—magazines, clubs, little theatres, art or free-love or single-tax colonies, experimental schools, picture galleries. Everywhere was a sense of secret companionship and immense potentialities for change.' If the brave new world envisaged by artists and social reformers was still mainly potentiality, the actuality appeared to be just round the corner of every city block; and continuing industrial expansion, if not always utopian in direction, was bringing about significant social changes.

New industrial developments not only multiplied both blue-collar and white-collar jobs but subtly altered the modes of urban life. Thus, as the invention of the mechanical refrigerator and the vast increase in the variety of inexpensive canned goods on grocers' shelves simplified 'light housekeeping', small families chose to eat at home instead of patronising city restaurants or living in boarding houses. When a method of fabricating standardised concrete building blocks gave the construction industry an economical, fireproof material, contractors began to put up substantial five- and six-storey apartment houses. Large-scale production of heavy-duty electric power transmission cables contributed to a dispersal of factories to sites supplied by truck rather than railroad. While the automobile industry spawned new companies to make such specialities as the self-starter and improved brake linings, the most revolutionary change in everyday life sprang from the nearly 2.5 million automobiles in use by 1915.

With automobiles at their doorsteps, some thousands of city dwellers turned into suburbanites, leaving their old city houses to be occupied by carless families or converted to commercial use. Beyond city limits, where cheaper land and lower taxes offered bait, new 'industrial parks' rose, with small houses in the vicinity to accommodate workmen's families in less cramped quarters than city tenements afforded. In the nearby 'central city', a term that would not come into common use for another generation, taxpayers welcomed this flight to the suburbs; it provided a safeguard against intolerable congestion. Massachusetts, in fact, established a Homestead Commission to encourage dispersion of population in a 'back to the land' movement, passed a city planning act in 1913, and early in 1915, following the examples set in Australia and New Zealand, authorised state purchase of land on which suitable housing for low-income families might rise. Unhappily, the dwellings built and sold at cost on long-term loans under this plan were few. State-financed garden towns failed to materialise. Private contractors built the houses in residential suburbs without adhering to any overall plan of community development. Meanwhile, new arrivals from rural areas or from Europe constantly fed into the old centres, an inflow that maintained the cities' population totals, but, because of its economic level, reduced per capita wealth. Still the big cities represented the stronghold of American financial power and American vitality. Outward migrations and perpetual shifts in the make-up of neighbourhoods seemed unlikely to weaken the position of the metropolitan centres.

The outbreak of war in Europe caused a brief business recession in the United States, and, despite a sharp drop in immigration, deepened antagonisms in the cities among foreign-born groups and between them and smug native-born who rejoiced that Americans were not as other men. Within a year, however, British and French war orders were reviving America's heavy industry. When the German submarine attacks on neutral shipping began, the pace of industrial production quickened. Detroit's automobile plants were hurriedly recruiting workmen months before the United States entered the war in the spring of 1917. Thereafter the necessity of tripling and quadrupling the output of cars, army trucks, and tracked vehicles, and starting upon manufacture of airplane engines led to the importation of Negroes from the South, for by then elaboration of assembly-line techniques had eliminated the need of skilled workmen on many jobs. Suddenly manpower shortages developed everywhere—in the aircraft plants opened in Seattle, in the shipyards from Maine to the far Northwest, in the rubber tyre factories in Akron, Ohio, in Pittsburgh's and Chicago's steel mills, and Cleveland's oil refineries. As the draft took young men off to army camps, the pressures rose higher. Although the farms needed hands to raise the foodstuffs for war-ridden, hungry Europe, the exodus from the agricultural areas to industrial centres went on.

This mass movement of people subsided within two and a half years, but in that interval it destroyed any possibility of restoring a balance between city and country. As a popular song put it after the Armistice: 'How you gonna keep 'em down on the farm after they've seen Paree?' Despite the meagre resemblance of an American industrial city to Paris, the same force worked on factory hands who had never before known city life of any kind. Families who moved from the Kentucky or North Carolina mountains or from farms in Mississippi and Arkansas to, say, Pittsburgh or Detroit or St. Louis were unwilling to return either during or after the war. Washington, headquarters of war planning and administration, experienced a similar permanent expansion; only part of the supposedly temporary throng of clerks and professional people returned to their former homes.

In all the war production centres lack of housing and the slow service of overburdened city transit systems were a first source of trouble. Although the federal government built several thousand houses for war workers' families and erected dormitories in Washington for unmarried clerks, the number of units met only a fraction of the demand, and some of them were not ready for occupancy till after the Armistice. In a few industrial communities company housing eased the pinch, but in scores of cities new arrivals had to squeeze into already overcrowded quarters. City health departments were unable to check the ravages of the peculiarly virulent epidemic of Spanish influenza that struck the United States in the early autumn of 1918; people died like flies. Wherever an inundation of Negro workers occurred, notably in Detroit, Chicago, and St Louis, racial friction deepened; East St Louis saw a full-scale riot. City school systems were severly handicapped by the resignation of teachers to take better-paying war jobs at the very moment that school enrolments were increasing. Still a sense of mission pervaded the hard-pressed cities; people felt they were 'doing their bit'. Although the *Chicago Tribune*, moulder of public opinion in much of the Mid-west, and Mayor 'Big Bill' Thompson, Chicago's Republican boss, consistently twisted the British lion's tail, in every city in the country 'Four-Minutemen' speaking at Liberty loan rallies, Red Cross volunteers making sanitary dressings in church halls and assembly rooms, and a flood of pamphlets setting forth America's war aims sustained belief that the United States was engaged in a holy crusade that would put Europe to rights and make a better world at home when the fighting was over.

Disillusionment set in as soon as the welcome-home parades for soldiers of the AEF came to an end early in 1919. With the cancellation of government contracts, war plants curtailed production, dismissed surplus employees, and slashed high wartime wage-rates, whereupon strikes set in from coast to coast, beginning in January with a general strike in Seattle. The 'Red Scare' that simultaneously enveloped the country worsened troubles; employers and metropolitan newspapers took the position that a Bolshevik conspiracy to destroy constitutional government was afoot in the United States. 'Reds' must have penetrated working men's ranks. What else could explain labour's new militance? Race riots in Washington and Chicago in the summer and distrust of the course of peace negotiations at Versailles strengthened the conviction of a considerable segment of the public that Americans, so far from making the world safe for democracy, had simply involved themselves in a struggle from which a return to 'normalcy' would be possible only by repressive measures.

Despite assumptions that labour radicalism underlay every disturbance, the outburst of racial warfare, whether a series of incidents or full-scale riots, was a by-product of the Negro migration into crowded Northern communities. In the capital the five days of intermittent street fighting were partly the aftermath of panic over a bomb set in the house of the Attorney General and over a number of sex crimes which white citizens atttibuted to Negroes, and partly, the police department believed, the result of a deliberate plot contrived by leaders of the white underworld to undermine police authority. In Chicago the riot began on the Lake Michigan bathing beaches at the end of a hot day; an eminent sociologist later propounded the theory that the mere physiological shock of seeing so many black bodies had awakened a primitive revulsion in white people. The conflict spread from the lake shore to every part of the city into which Negro families had recently moved. Later investigation showed that police unwillingness to protect coloured people had turned a fracas into a war; and behind that lay the all-encompassing fact that since the late 1860s white Americans, Northerners and Southerners alike, had consistently either ignored or exploited Negroes. While the chapters of the National Association for the Advancement of Colored People and the Chicago Urban League strove to create understanding between the races, a majority of white people, once order was restored, dismissed the problem from mind.

On the industrial front the battles were novel only because they affected virtually all industry and were sustained with peculiar intensity. Yet no disorder attended Seattle's general strike. Engineered by local unions of the AFL to display their disciplined strength to employers, the five-day demonstration consisted solely of cutting off all services in the city except milk deliveries to households with small children, laundry work at the city's hospitals, operation of the municipal lighting plant, and handling the United States mails. Then, without making any specific demands, workmen went back to their jobs. The manœuvre miscarried; employers and citizens not directly involved persisted in thinking it a preliminary to a Bolshevik-inspired revolution. Similar fears pervaded Mid-western cities where violence broke out on the picket lines around steel plants during a country-wide steel strike. When Boston's underpaid and overworked police force struck, outraged Americans in all industrial areas regarded the threat to law and order as further evidence of subversive influences at work. After the strikers agreed to return to duty, Governor Calvin Coolidge's denunciation of the short-lived rebellion made him a national figure, elected him to the Vice-Presidency of the United States a year later, and put him into the White House upon President Harding's death in 1923. Meanwhile the Federal Bureau of Investigation, its prestige enormously enhanced by its vigorous anti-Red drives, arrested obscure 'radicals' among workmen in cities all over the country, while a panicky Congress rushed through an emergency anti-immigration act. The Red Scare fortunately petered out in 1921. But by then labour's fight for collective bargaining had also collapsed.

If the 'money power' and the urban middle classes felt reassured by their triumph over radicalism, a carry-over from the Red Scare united them in demanding that city school systems expand 'Americanisation' classes and in clamouring for permanent immigration restrictions. Even industrialists who wanted a renewed supply of cheap labour shunned the risk of a fresh invasion of 'Reds'. Labour union members practically to a man advocated closing the doors. The law passed in 1924 set up a quota system nationality by nationality which sharply reduced the numbers who could enter from eastern and southern Europe. Only after the stream of newcomers shrank to the 150,000 a year allowed by the new law did city dwellers begin to acknowledge that the varied cultural backgrounds of the foreign-born had enriched American life.

By the end of the 1920s most of the foreign-language colonies in the big cities had lost much of their one-time cohesiveness, although it endured sufficiently in the realm of politics to force election analysts to take into account 'the Italian vote', 'the Polish vote', and the like. It was the presidential campaign of 1928 that first drew naturalised immigrants into the national political arena, for Al Smith, New York-born, Roman Catholic, and son of an Irish mother, appealed to them as one of their own. In most respects, however, members of the first generation born in this country were determined to be like everybody else and therefore to discard parental folkways. Only here and there would pride of origin preserve some of the Old World customs. Within the bounds of Detroit, for example, Hamtramck survived as an independent city of Polish-Americans who spoke Polish more often than English, celebrated Polish festivals, and wore Polish peasant dress on holidays. Polish and Russian Orthodox Jews were among the exceptions that, in clinging to their orthodoxy, perpetuated separate enclaves. German Jews who had come a generation or two before, particularly those who had moved up the economic and social ladder, had often joined Protestant churches, perhaps initially because observance of Jewish dietary laws was difficult or because the easiest way to avoid anti-Semitism was to drop the religious differentiation; those who accepted Reformed Judaism, moreover, soon lost distinctive modes of dress and behaviour. Still conservative and orthodox Jewish congregations outnumbered Reformed; in sections of New York, Baltimore, St. Louis, Chicago, and a few other cosmopolitan communities the long beard, the black skull cap, and the robe of the orthodox rabbi were still a commonplace when World War II broke out.

Meanwhile the expectations of city workmen that they would profit from curtailed immigration met with disappointment. Although a tremendous boom succeeded the post-war years of strikes and business recession, the undiminished supply of industrial labour, now recruited not from Europe but from American farms and villages, left wage earners insecure. Census figures tell part of the story: the 17,688,000 non-farm householders in the United States in 1920 grew to 23,266,000 by 1930, whereas farm families, numbering 6,790,000 in 1920, dropped to 6,729,000. Veterans returned from overseas and their brief taste of 'Paree' made up only a small part of the stream flowing citywards, and, while not all erstwhile country folk turned into industrial workers, their numbers constituted an added threat to men already worried over increasing mechanisation in industry. When the Ford Company closed down its plants near Detroit to re-tool for a new model in 1927, nine months without pay reduced Ford workmen to docility. A Massachusetts textile mill strike boomeranged when the company installed automatic machines manned by a half dozen hands to do the work formerly performed by a hundred or more. Automation, which in another thirty years would throw several million people out of work, was already a dread possibility.

New industries, on the other hand, some of them born in industrial laboratories, created new jobs. By the mid-1920s products rarely heard of or totally unknown before the war were pouring out of new factories or re-equipped old. Although companies sometimes built plants in small towns where real estate prices and taxes were relatively low and the prospects of recruiting cheap labour were good, a great many new enterprises located in or on the outskirts of cities, perhaps because employees at the management level preferred the bright lights of the city, or because, trucking notwithstanding, transport was simpler in railroad centres. Manufacturing corporations almost invariably maintained sales offices in a big city, even when their factories were elsewhere. Merchandising and familiarising the public with novel, improved, or cheapened wares became special arts whose mysteries called for courses of study at universities and business schools. As advertising took on new importance, New York's Madison Avenue came to be the headquarters of a glamorous selling profession. Young men fresh out of college found green pastures in the terrain of city brokerage houses selling shares in the new companies and in long-established 'blue chip' enterprises. When the big bull market brought in customers who had never before 'played the big board', stockbrokers garnered fat commissions merely by sitting within reach of their telephones. Wall Street and LaSalle Street firms found it well worth their while to open branch offices in small cities. At the same time a vast urban real estate and building boom opened still another path to quick riches or at least to well-paid employment.

Some of this prosperity brushed off upon wage earners. Although industrial management usually insisted either upon the 'open shop' or company unions, still pay rates were generally somewhat higher than in pre-war years. Steel workers in Pittsburgh and Chicago, it is true, averaged only $28.00 for a seventy-hour week, and at cotton mills in Gastonia, North Carolina, pay rates of $18.00 for men, $9.00 for women, still less for the fourteen-year-olds who worked a sixty-six-hour week caused a bloody strike in 1928. But in most industries in Northern and Western cities all classes of society had more to spend and spent it more freely than ever before. Inasmuch as profits from mass production depended upon mass consumption, prices for articles considered luxuries by the rest of the world stayed within the reach of American wage earners, particularly as city retailers advertised, 'Buy now, pay later'.

Instalment buying came to be a normal procedure. It enabled people dependent on weekly wages to invest in refrigerators, radios, and automobiles. It made the 4·8 million cars produced in 1929 seem a reasonable output, for not only in Detroit but in cities all over the country, factory hands, like executives, drove cars to work. As the American woman became 'America's greatest fur-bearing animal', tales told of Chicago typists and clerks earning perhaps $20.00 a week who 'bought' new fur coats every December by making a small down payment and modest monthly remittances until in April the bill collector reclaimed the coat; the next winter other furriers would accept the risks. *Caveat vendor*. The city house-holder, however, relied increasingly upon 'cash and carry' chain stores where prices were cheaper than at independent grocers' and butchers' shops. Before the end of the 1920s chain stores handled two-thirds of the food sales in Philadelphia, 35 per cent of all Chicago's retail sales, 22 per cent of Baltimore's.

City dwellers always seemed to find money for the cinema. As movie-going became a standard pastime, neighbourhood movie houses proliferated while huge, elaborately decorated theatres opened downtown to show, for a price, Hollywood's latest pictures. By the end of the 1920s movie theatres were selling 100 million seats weekly. Facts and fiction about the private lives of movie stars filled gossip columns in metropolitan newspapers and made movie magazines a staple article of merchandise at corner drug stores and

E

news-stands. Only the sports world attracted comparable attention. Though nothing else competed with baseball, other spectator sports —boxing, professional football, and ice hockey—also commanded big audiences, irrespective of the cost of admission. When some 91,000 people crowded into Boyles' Thirty Acres in Jersey City to watch Jack Dempsey fight 'gorgeous' Georges Carpentier, the take at the gate was over $1 million. College football games, once attended chiefly by students and alumni, drew from cities within a 150-mile radius onlookers who had never seen or wanted to see the inside of a college library or lecture hall. Mass entertainment for the urban masses of the 1920s was at least dissimilar from the Roman circuses in that Americans spent their own or their creditors' money for diversion. Neither poor people nor rich worried about spending today; tomorrow promised more. For all its slightly bawdy tone, a popular song of the period ticked off much of the urban scene: 'The rich get richer, and the poor get children. And in the mean-time, and in between time, ain't we got fun!'

During part of the year the very rich still occupied their great mansions along New York's Fifth Avenue, Philadelphia's Ritten-house Square, Chicago's Lake Shore Drive, and San Francisco's Nob Hill and Russian Hill, but they spent less time in the city than formerly and more at their country places or in Europe. Huge blocks of luxury flats, moreover, began to rise to accommodate the newly rich and the well-to-do unwilling to struggle with the 'Servant Problem' in a society so affluent that a servant class, no longer renewed by immigration, was rapidly disappearing. Mean-while, although the exodus of permanent residents, especially middle-class families with children, continued to build up 'bed-room' suburbs, city populations grew. In 1920 New York, Chicago, and Philadelphia each contained over a million inhabitants; within a decade Detroit and Los Angeles, metropolis of the mushrooming movie industry, reached that total, and nine cities, in contrast to five in 1910, had over a half million residents.

More bodies meant bigger municipal budgets. While the building boom in apartment houses, big hotels, stores, and solid blocks of offices brought in new revenue to city treasuries, demands for public services expanded still faster. The reason was presumably twofold:

first, the disproportionate number of the unemployed and unemployables of metropolitan areas who lived in the cities and, second, the insistence of city taxpayers, confronted with constantly
rising assessments, that they get more for their money. Citizens
once tolerant of 'boodle' payments and palm greasing in the city
hall now began to watch municipal expenditures. Transit needs
constantly caused trouble. Caught by the long-term franchises
granted earlier to traction and utility companies, scores of cities had
to acquiesce in fare increases. Municipally owned lines also came
under fire. If the necessity of meticulous street cleaning declined
with the disappearance of horse-drawn vehicles, every other municipal want intensified.

City councilmen doubtless would have preferred to carry on
under the old regime of political bosses who dished out favours to
their henchmen and milked everyone else, but that system was hard
to maintain when voters began to clamour for new schools and new
highways and better protection from hoodlums. Thus some of the
goals for which Progressives and do-gooders had striven for a quarter
of a century came within reach in the mid-1920s. In city after city
blatant corruption faded into the background as the old machine
politicians lost their assurance of re-election. After immigration
restriction reduced the crop of newly naturalised citizens, bosses
dared not count on solid blocks of foreign-born votes. More important, with such an organisation as the American Civic Association
and its chapters in fifty cities hammering away at well-educated,
conscientious, socially secure men to run for office, neglect of the
public interest, let alone outright stealing from the public purse,
became increasingly risky.

In an era when bootleggers directed by crime syndicates were
building up great regional networks, the task of reforming city
government would seem to have been hopeless. But to an astonishing degree it took hold, sometimes with the help of new city charters and state laws granting municipalities wider powers, sometimes
solely by using existing machinery in charge of civic-minded
officials. The movement to get rid of grafters, begun in 1914 and
1915 but then halted by the war, regained impetus about 1926. A
number of communities, tired of incompetence and squabbling,

installed city managers at good salaries and with extensive authority. In this civic renaissance the League of Women Voters played a part. Born in 1920 after ratification of the Woman Suffrage Amendment, the League organised chapters in cities throughout the country, embarked on a vigorous campaign of voter education, and, by means of careful studies of significant local and national problems, infused fresh vitality into the search for workable solutions. Lord Bryce's criticisms of 1888 and the muckrakers' revelations had little relevance to American municipal government at the end of the 1920s, except in New York and three or four other cities. Only in policing were there disastrous lapses.

The lawlessness bred by Prohibition constituted the major threat to orderly government at every level. Otherwise law-abiding citizens, outraged at this denial of what they deemed their rights as individuals, made bathtub gin, patronised speakeasies, and defiantly dealt with bootleggers. Liquor consumption rose to heights unimagined in 1917, even affecting country towns in the bone-dry rural sections whose representatives had rammed the amendment through Congress and ratifying state legislatures. If champions of the measure considered it a rebuke to the wicked city, a wholesome reminder that rural virtues and rural values still exercised power in the United States, they suffered none the less from the backlash. Yet one of the reasons for Al Smith's defeat in 1928 was his endorsement of repeal of the Prohibition amendment. 'Rum, Romanism', and, to spoil the alliteration, his urban origins and point of view made him anathema to the teetotallers of the Protestant 'Bible belt'. Whether city repudiation of the dry law inspired the excessive hedonism of the 1920s or was itself a by-product of a 'vast dissolution of ancient habits', the results were the same, and far-reaching.

Criminals acquired fortunes and thus power such as even the pirates along the Gulf coast and 'black-birders' of slave smuggling days had never enjoyed. 'Al' Capone organised gangsters in Chicago and established an underworld on so permanent a basis that forty years later the forces of good city government were still combating it. Ties with gangs in other cities were close. In New Orleans the Mafia flourished, headed, rumour ran, by descendants of the Sicilian immigrants of the 1880s. Along with rum-running, gangsters conducted thriving businesses in gambling, prostitution, and narcotics peddling. Police officers often connived with the gangs. In New York City that situation would continue until an investigation authorised by Governor Franklin D. Roosevelt and conducted by the fearless Judge Seabury in 1931 ousted some of the most unsavoury local officials and the next year ended the public career of the charming, irresponsible, and thoroughly corrupt Mayor 'Jimmie' Walker. Whether news broadcasts, by keeping Americans informed of what was going on about them in the 1920s, lessened the reach of the criminal explosion is uncertain. Probably small cities escaped the worst of it because they were too small to yield the syndicates rich rewards.

While criminal violence spread, the methods of handling the misfits and derelicts of urban society underwent little change despite wider use of case work techniques and professionally trained social workers in public welfare departments. Bridewells, twentieth-century variations of nineteenth-century poorhouses, and municipal hospitals expanded, and states enlarged penal institutions and asylums for the insane and feeble-minded, but in contrast to the $1,295 million that local governments spent on highways in 1927, public welfare netted $111 million. Voluntary associations still took charge of the bulk of welfare services—child-care centres, settlement houses, family counselling, employment bureaus, legal aid, and, through Community Chests or Associated Charities, direct relief in the form of food, clothing, and fuel. And voluntary gifts were generous.

A growing number of foundations headed by competent and dedicated 'philanthropoids' undertook some long-term projects aimed at preventing social ills. The Rockefeller Foundation, for example, supported medical research and public health programmes, the Russell Sage Foundation regional and community planning. But the directors of particular city charities, whether homes for the aged or children's hospitals, rarely spent intensive effort on devising social reforms calculated to forestall dependency and want. A thoughtless public tended to characterise professional social workers as 'officious and ground-grippered or . . . repressed and revolutionary'. Any proposal for new social legislation met with opposition from businessmen, politicians, and even churchmen. As churches representing 'organised altruism' reinterpreted the Social Gospel of Washington Gladden, William Rainsford, and their contemporaries, church swimming pools, game rooms, and gymnasiums opened where parishioners and their protégés could breathe 'the oxygen of good fellowship'. Pastors attuned to the times took advertising slogans for sermon titles: 'Three-in-One Oil' referring to the Trinity, 'Eventually, Why Not Now?', an exhortation to conversion. If small-town churches were scandalised at such worldliness, their protests did not affect America's cities. In the observation of an astute New York congressman, social security propositions seemed faintly ridiculous to a nation that 'believed in the dogma of eternal prosperity'.

As befitted an affluent society, interest in good public schools, on the other hand, rose. Progressive education, as John Dewey had used the term in 1899, meant education constantly adjusted to a changing society, schooling that would preserve in a mechanised world the most important values of a vanishing rural civilisation. In the 1920s educators embraced the philosophy with enthusiasm. Unfortunately, misunderstandings of Dewey's ideas led some schools, especially private progressive schools, to insist that permissiveness was all-important and to abandon such disciplines as memorising the multiplication tables or the sequence of the letters of the alphabet. But while complainants declared that children now learned only what they wanted to, newly organised research departments in big city school systems and in those of well-to-do suburbs introduced intelligence and achievement testing and tabulated the results of experiments in teaching methods. The outcome was a distinct improvement in the quality of education offered. Smaller communities were then able to adopt the proven techniques. Furthermore, better enforced attendance laws and more years of schooling exposed pupils to a larger body of knowledge than at the turn of the century. Whereas in 1900 a city child had one chance in ten of going to high school and one in thirty-three of entering college, by 1930 he had one chance in two for high school, one in seven for college. At the same time health supervision broadened. Dental clinics and eye tests came to be almost a matter of course, budgets for school doctors and nurses increased, and physical education received new emphasis. In keeping with American dedication to spectator sport, parents insisted upon high-school gymnasiums and ball fields: a school without a football and basketball team hardly ranked as a school at all. And as junior high schools became part of the educational system, only those in slum sections were denied space and equipment for organised recreation.

Civic pride, fortifying notions of convenience, also asserted itself in building parkways to speed automobile traffic through business districts and out to residential areas, while highway engineers and planners paid at least lip service to urban beauty. In Washington the federal government created a National Capital Park and Planning Commission to purchase land for parks and scenic drives and embarked upon an elaborate scheme of building and landscaping. Along the Hudson River, New York City completed a two-level parkway below the heights of Riverside Drive; in lower Manhattan, realtors bought up office buildings, replaced them with seventy-storeyed skyscrapers, and ran the Empire State Building to 102 storeys. Here was a model. In the vast spaces of the Great Plains, Tulsa and Oklahoma City, scarcely more than villages before the discovery of oil in the region early in the century, burst forth with skyscrapers and parkways. Chicago undertook the long-talked-of lake-shore development with a stadium, fountains, and acres of automobile parking laid out to the south of the Art Institute, an 'outer drive' to the east stretching from the site of the 1893 World's Fair to the far north side, and a new natural history museum and a planetarium built on made-up land along the lake front formerly pre-empted by the Illinois Central Railroad tracks. The heavy tower of the Chicago Tribune Building rose to fifty-two storeys on Michigan Avenue; nearby on the Chicago River, where the wholesale vegetable and fish markets had stood, Samuel Insull, transit tycoon, erected an imposing opera house; and across the river Marshall Field & Company built a mighty Merchandise Mart.

'As I caught my first glimpse of Detroit,' wrote a British worshipper of Henry Ford's genius, 'I felt as I imagine a Seventeenth Century traveller must have felt when he approached Versailles.' Yet perhaps no city better exemplified the consequences of sacrificing everything to the automobile. Hundred-year-old elms and maples came down to make space for many-laned highways obliterating the circles which Augustus Woodward had laid out for the frontier town of 1803. Now towering office buildings crowded the stretches near the waterfront or stood cheek by jowl with low-profiled automobile plants flanked fore and aft by asphalt parking lots. While much of the central business district exuded an aura of massive power, from there outwards the miles of repair shops, tacky-looking stores, and squat apartment-house blocks conveyed a sense of irredeemable drabness. Pleasant houses set in wide lawns that lined quiet streets as late as 1920 disappeared before 1930.

Small cities widened streets, while oil companies erected gas stations on corners where for decades ornamental iron or picket fences around roomy old houses had fended off the vulgar. Newport, in the 1920s as much Navy base as millionaire summer resort, let honky tonks patronised by sailors crowd in upon Peter Harrison's eighteenth-century edifices and the shabby, beautiful houses of colonial merchants; but she paved and maintained Ocean Drive and the avenues bordered by palatial late nineteenth-century summer 'cottages'. The only places untouched by this brand of urban improvement were those already experiencing the blight of unemployment—New England textile towns such as New Bedford, one-time mainstay of Massachusetts' whaling and then of her fine-cotton industry, Pennsylvania mining communities rendered hopeless by the switch from coal to fuel oil, and a few Southern cities too unsure of their industrial future to risk the expense of sweeping change.

Yet all the building and rebuilding, in the opinion of a good many observers, was not creating viable communities and was certainly not providing proper housing for city families with low incomes. In 1919 Governor Alfred E. Smith of New York appointed a state reconstruction commission and a housing committee to study the problem. Three years later, while Milwaukee set an example by investing municipal funds in shares in a 'limited dividend' low-cost housing project, Andrew J. Thomas of New York achieved the first break-through in apartment-house design. Each unit of the 2,000-family development he built for the Metropolitan Life Insurance Company opened out upon a spacious central court; the

tax exemption the state and city granted limited dividend enterprises of this sort kept maximum rentals to $9 a month per room.
This success led John D. Rockefeller, Jr, to engage Thomas to build
other garden apartments in New York and persuaded Chicago
philanthropists concerned with housing to adopt the plan.

Meanwhile, under the leadership of the dynamic New York
architect Clarence Stein, a small group of architects, economists,
conservationists, and biosociologists founded the Regional Planning
Association of America. The menace to American civilisation,
wrote one member, lay not in the urban environment, but in the
metropolitan environment created by the railroad and steam
engine. Intelligent use of electric power transmission and motor
transport could, however, effect a redistribution of population and
industry; the regional city could replace the 'congealed massing' of
metropolitanism, where humanity was 'void of social structure,
unbound by geographic confines, and uninspired by any common
interest'. In order to accomplish that goal, a report prepared in 1925
by Lewis Mumford of Columbia University declared that hence-
forward city building must proceed within a new institutional
framework: the architect, the planner, and the welfare expert,
instead of the real estate speculator, the commercial promoter, and
the highway engineer, should fix policies; human dignity and comfort rather than contractors' profits must determine the character of
developments. Clarence Stein and the talented Henry Wright were
already providing model planned communities that combined convenience and architectural charm at moderate cost. Unhappily
Sunnyside Gardens on Long Island, for all its ingenious planning,
had to charge rentals above truly low-cost standards, and Radburn
on the Hackensack meadows below Jersey City, because finished
after the depression set in, was financially unsuccessful. A third
project, the beautifully designed Chatham Village, located two miles
from the heart of Pittsburgh, accommodated higher-income families
and thus escaped monetary difficulties. But all three demonstrated
the Regional Planning Associations' theses. In the mid-1930s the
association's principles would form the basis for several New Deal
undertakings.

While urban sociologists, notably Robert Park and his disciples

F

at the University of Chicago, turned out informing empirical studies of the forces operating in the big cities, and Robert and Helen Lynd's *Middletown* dissected the small Mid-western city, courageous academic economists explored the blind spots of big business and John Dewey re-examined the problem of social disorganisation. Not content merely to analyse 'the frantic search to fill the void caused by the loosening of the bonds which hold persons together in the immediate community of experience', Dewey sought a remedy; a larger volume of well-informed reading matter pouring out from an enlightened press could, he argued, restore direct human communication. The book-publishing press preferred to publish the novels of the 'Lost Generation'. Those ignored the city as such. *Winesburg, Ohio, Main Street,* and *Babbit* attacked the small town; Dos Passos in *U.S.A.* lashed out at everything shoddy in America; the others wrote of themselves and a world in which they found 'all Gods dead, all wars fought, all faiths in man shaken'.

In response to homespun critics of the era who expostulated over the deterioration or city morals, the jazz broadcasts that they felt were corrupting musical taste, and the 'meaninglessness' or indecency of the modernistic paintings and sculpture on exhibit in metropolitan show rooms, an occasional defender pointed out that city people had merely abandoned hypocrisy; that they at least had learned to listen to music daily; the 'Gentleman Dealers in Second Hand Thoughts', in the poet E. E. Cummings' phrase, could not judge the exhilaration of John Marin's 'Mountain Top', or the sharp planes of shadow and light in Charles Sheeler's 'Church Street El', perhaps still less Grant Wood's 'American Gothic'; that in contrast to the lifelessness of earlier American sculpture, Gaston Lachaise's voluptuous 'Woman' was 'magnificently conjugated largeness'. Most city dwellers saw no reason either to attack or defend the pleasures prosperity opened up to them. If the $8 million worth of 'art' imported from Great Britain in a single year be an indication, among those pleasures was looking at paintings and *objets d'art*, good or bad.

Although Hollywood and broadcasting stations largely determined the tastes and opinions of Americans from New York and

San Francisco to Duluth and Galveston, pockets of resistance held out in the country. In 1926 university communities were shaken by the Scopes' trial, at which rural Tennesseeans successfully upheld the religious fundamentalism that banned the teaching of evolution in the public schools of the state, but urbanites generally dismissed the matter as a joke; such antiquities could not long withstand the power of the city.

Neither hedonists, fundamentalists, troubled intellectuals, nor artists dismayed at the ugliness of urban America foresaw in the summer of 1929 how quickly and completely the 'Era of Wonderful Nonsense' would vanish. Prices on the New York Stock Exchange slipped downward in September, rallied, and then tumbled precipitately in late October. Investment bankers and industrialists whistling to keep their courage up insisted for several months that here was merely a temporary dip in the business cycle, but the spring of 1930 stilled those assurances. It was as if someone had turned a light switch and cut off the current. During the next three years, while mortgage foreclosures cost farmers their land and city workmen their homes, savings evaporated, banks closed, and brokers jumped out of windows on Wall Street. Industrial giants slashed payrolls, reduced operations to a few hours a week, and sometimes shut down their plants altogether. The 6 million unemployed in 1930 rose with every passing month; an average of 100,000 workers were fired weekly during the next two years. In 1932 New York City alone had a million jobless, Chicago 660,000; 80 per cent of Toledo's working people were unemployed, 60 per cent of Akron's, 50 per cent of Cleveland's. In deserted factory buildings and empty stores, sweatshops opened where thirteen-year-olds might earn 20 to 50 cents for a day's work.

The richest municipalities staggered under the mounting burdens. Private charities, their resources constantly dwindling, were unable to maintain their customary services, let alone expand them. A hundred cities provided the unemployed with no public assistance of any kind. In 1932, urged on by Milwaukee's old-line socialist Mayor Victor Berger and Governor Robert La Follette, Wisconsin enacted an unemployment compensation law that eased matters for working people, but the plan was too new to operate smoothly and employers themselves were financially hard-pressed. New York City's Welfare Department limited relief payments to $2.39 a week per family; St Louis cut her relief rolls in half; New Orleans refused all new applicants for help. When Detroit, barred from taxing the Ford and Chrysler factories because they were outside the city limits, sought to borrow from the companies, the companies made the loans on condition that the city slash the relief rolls by a third, although workmen fired from the automobile plants made up a sizeable proportion of the Detroiters on relief. Richmond, Knoxville, and Atlanta resorted to printing local scrip to serve as emergency currency. Adolescents unable to get work enrolled in city high schools at a time when shrinking budgets were threatening the very survival of public education. Alabama closed 85 per cent of her schools. In other states scores of communities shortened the school year from nine to seven months. Most cities cut teachers' salaries in half. New York dismissed 11,000 teachers. Chicago teachers went for months with no pay at all; salary arrears ran to $28 million before the end of 1932.

In hopes of halting the downward spiral, the federal government first set up a Reconstruction Finance Corporation to lend money to banks, railroads, and building and loan associations, and six months later authorised loans to municipalities for public works that would check unemployment. But the RFC moved cautiously. Cities cut down on building projects. Except in Washington where the federal building programme provided work for nearly 10,000 men, this type of work relief proved an ineffectual stop-gap. 'Hoovervilles' of makeshift shanties housing families evicted from their homes began to crop up in every city; in New York's Central Park a drained reservoir became 'Hoover Valley'. Children dug for food in St Louis's garbage dump; men and women hung around back doors of Chicago restaurants to pick up scraps; queues of hungry people lined up at 'soup kitchens' wherever they existed. Bands of men and boys took 'to the road'; estimates put the number drifting from place to place at some 2 million aimlessly looking for a livelihood.

Concluding that the federal government could and must give direct help, in the early summer of 1932 some 20,000 World War I veterans converged on Washington to ask Congress to pay out immediately the bonus due to them in 1945 for their service in 1917 and 1918. The 'Bonus Expeditionary Force', swelled by some of the marchers' families, totalled close to 60,000 before the end of June. They encamped in empty buildings at the foot of Capitol Hill and on the mud flats of the city dump. For the first time within Washingtonians' memory, they saw white men and Negroes amicably sharing quarters and their meagre rations. When the Senate rejected the bonus bill, about 15,000 of the marchers decided to stay on till Congress reversed the decision. Why go back to non-existent homes and non-existent jobs? The dispersal came when Army regulars, acting upon the orders of President Hoover's Secretary of War, drove them from their temporary billets near the Capitol and set fire to the tar-paper camp on the dump. Americans' shock of this cavalier treatment contributed to Hoover's defeat in the presidential election in November.

Anger and hopelessness dominated the mood of the United States as 1933 dawned. People were doubtful whether President-elect Franklin Delano Roosevelt, for all his campaign promises, could pull the nation out of the morass. Metropolitan newspapers and journals were gloomy. Nearly 13·8 million Americans were out of work and their savings exhausted. As malnutrition and disease raised the death rate, the urban birth rate dropped. Young married couples doubled up with their parents in order to save expenses. City householders who had grown up in the country and still had relatives there returned to the farms and villages. On city streets lined with boarded-up shops purse-snatchings and hold-ups became commonplaces, while political radicals contended that only recourse to communism could save the country. 'Of all the losses wrought by the depression,' remarked one writer, 'the ebullient optimism of 1914 was the chief casualty.'

7

EFFECTS OF THE NEW DEAL AND WAR

On the dark morning of March 4, 1933, a frightened nation waited anxiously, wondering whether its social and political institutions could survive with more than 12 million people out of work, every bank in the United States closed, hunger stalking the city streets, and the means of relief seemingly exhausted. What hope could the new President hold out? The answer came suddenly with apocalyptic force. As Franklin Delano Roosevelt's inaugural address sounded out over the Capitol Plaza in Washington and to radio listeners throughout the country, Americans experienced a rebirth of faith. Built on the assurance that 'we have nothing to fear but fear itself', that faith never wavered thereafter. It would surmount the bitter quarrels and uncertainties that lay ahead, the periods of class warfare in industrial and commercial centres, and ultimately the strains of global war.

As the paralysis of banking and destruction of credit was the most critical problem of the moment, on March 9 an Emergency Banking Act passed both houses of Congress and received the President's signature in less than nine hours. It had the effect of switching on the current that had stopped in 1930. An issue of 2 million $1,000 Federal Reserve notes enabled banks to reopen under Treasury licenses and surveillance and brought gold and deposits flowing back into circulation. In what a London journal called a 'lurch into State socialism', Congress enacted fourteen other major bills before the middle of June. The laws most directly important to city dwellers were the Federal Emergency Relief Act which set up a national relief system; the act establishing a Civilian Conservation Corps to take jobless boys and young men from the city streets and put them to work on the public domain; the Home Owners' Loan Act providing refinancing of home mortgages; an act guaranteeing bank deposits; and the National Industrial Recovery Act which called for a $3·3 billion public works programme and a system of industrial self-government and collective bargaining under federal supervision.

Two reports prepared by The National Resources Committee several years later clearly reflect the attitudes of New Deal policymakers towards the city. The special importance they attached to the well-being of urban communities emerged in a single paragraph summarising statistically the extent to which urban activities governed the life and livelihood of the entire country:

> Urbanization and suburbanization have meant . . . a centralization of enterprise in the Nation's cities, metropolitan districts, urban satellites, and industrial areas. Of more than 3,000 counties of the country, the 155 which contain the larger industrial cities embraced, in the year 1929, 74 per cent of all industrial wage earners, 81 per cent of all salaried employees, 79 per cent of all wages paid, 83 per cent of all salaries paid, 65 per cent of all the industrial establishments and 80 per cent of the value added to manufactured products. . . . The counties containing the 11 largest cities in the country accounted for over half of the wholesale trade, while the 93 cities over 100,000 reported three-fourths of the total.

Institutions and instruments of social guidance to facilitate and regulate urban life were essential, 'if only to keep the seething millions from trampling one another down in the workaday urban world'. Members of Congress representing rural constituencies saw to it that farm relief got full consideration, but of necessity the city received more attention than the national government or the states had ever accorded it before.

During the spring of 1933 as the Congressional legislation of the 'First Hundred Days' pumped vigour into the economy, industrial companies in a rush of fresh confidence placed orders for raw materials, while municipal engineers and school boards began to map out highway and sanitary projects and school buildings for which they could reasonably expect to get funds from the Public Works Administration in Washington. But the pump-priming that would eventually start up the machinery of industry and commerce and thus put people back to work could not and did not provide jobs overnight. The 12 million or more Americans who had been unemployed for months or years needed immediate help. Neither state nor municipal governments nor private charity could give it. Hunger-ridden families could not wait for public works programmes. In this situation the newly established Federal Emergency Relief Administration lost no time. Two days after its director, Harry Hopkins, took charge in May, part of the $500 million voted for grants-in-aid to the states was in the hands of state welfare agencies, while Hopkins, himself an experienced social worker, prepared to send trained staffs to organise relief in communities that lacked qualified social workers. By the fall, unwilling to see people subjected to the humiliation of receiving a dole if any other system were possible, Hopkins won approval for a national work relief scheme. Before the end of January 1934, over 4 million men and women were at work—men building airports for 500 cities, laying sewer lines, tidying up parks and playgrounds, women teaching adult classes in city school rooms. But as the programme was extremely costly and a certain amount of corruption crept in, funds for this form of work relief were cut off before the spring.

Fortunately the Public Works Administration had by then begun upon some of its major projects. A loan to the Pennsylvania Railroad enabled the company to finish the huge 30th Street Station in Philadelphia. A loan-grant provided Chicago with a new sewage system, New York with the Triborough Bridge, Kansas City with a municipal auditorium, Denver with a water supply system, the University of Washington in Seattle with new buildings. By 1939 the $6 billion spent by PWA had built new school houses in cities and towns all over the country, sewage disposal plants, hospitals, subways, bridges, court houses, and city halls. Once started, the projects offered Americans over 592 million days of work, and in the process improved the appearance of cities from coast to coast. At the peak of its activities, however, PWA could take up only part of the slack in employment; much of the work required special skills.

During the winter of 1934-5, although private industry and commerce were showing signs of recovery, city relief rolls were as long as those of the year before. The plight of the oldster was particularly grim. As part of a farm household he could perform useful chores and there was always room for him. In the city neither situation obtained. Obviously public enterprises must still create jobs for the able-bodied unemployables. But who was to contrive the jobs and who pay for the helpless? To the first question the answer was the Works Progress Administration, to the second, the acts inaugurating what Americans call loosely 'social security'— unemployment compensation; old-age insurance financed by payments shared equally by employer and employee; through a public assistance programme to be met from the federal and states' purses, pensions for the blind, for dependent children, for the disabled, and for the needy aged, and health services to mothers and children. The acts had drawbacks. While social security administrators in regional and municipal offices supplied some public assistance to the indigent aged and disabled, payments to people upon retirement would not begin until the 1940s, and unemployment insurance, arranged state by state, ordinarily applied only to persons who had jobs. Nevertheless, the non-salaried Board of Public Welfare in the District of Columbia probably spoke for similar bodies in all American cities in voicing its 'sense of the vast and enduring significance' of measures that 'represent the acceptance of the principle that government is responsible for at least a minimum of economic security for all its citizens'.

The Works Progress Administration was never able to meet all the demands upon it during its six years of life. Rigid rules governing who could qualify for local WPA assistance left out thousands of families in desperate straits. Some work assignments, furthermore, were intrinsically futile and ill-suited to the individuals given them. Projects such as leaf-raking in city parks, or patching pot holes in pavements, or clearing streets of snow evoked criticism from taxpayers who complained that WPA workers spent more time leaning on their rakes and shovels than using them; irritated observers rarely realised that at least half the men on the job were tubercular or ridden by other disease. Although local governments increased the $405 million spent out of local funds for relief in 1936 to some $629 million in 1940, the staffs of municipal welfare departments knew that without the federally subsidised make-work scheme local relief would have collapsed under the burden of trying to prevent starvation.

Nor was manual labour the only type of job the WPA provided. Indeed, in finding useful tasks for professional people and office workers, the WPA programme achieved a success of enduring importance. Assignment of jobless teachers and clerks to putting public school records in order helped in revitalising school systems, just as Public Works Administration funds for new school houses eased school budgets enough to permit re-hiring of teachers. Men and women with archival training assembled data on churches and American paintings, while the Federal Writers Project engaged historians and newspapermen in preparing guide books to every state in the Union and to New Orleans, Cincinnati, and Washington, D.C. Thirty years later the published volumes were still in constant use, and some of them had become collectors' items. The WPA Music Project helped organise city orchestras and choral societies. The Federal Theatre Project employed actors, directors, and stage designers in presenting plays, a number of them written for the purpose. Painters and sculptors took part in the Public Works of Art project which commissioned murals and other decorative art in post offices, city halls, and court houses the country over. For the first time, under the sponsorship of the WPA Art Project, Negro painters won recognition; Jacob Laurence's 'Firewood' and 'Migration of the Negro' series, for example, gave him an assured place among American artists. Intensely aware of conditions about them, many painters concentrated on 'social art', perhaps nowhere more effectively expressed than in Ben Shahn's mural in the Bronx Post Office for which, shown in the panels of common people at work, Walt Whitman's line supplied the theme: 'Democracy rests finally upon us.'

The effect was threefold: people with special talents unsuited to ditch digging were able to survive with dignity, the creative arts won an officially recognised place in American life, and, as much of the music, drama, and painting was open to the public free or at minimal prices, the 'man in the street' found enjoyment in things that had long seemed out of his reach. Audiences that had never before seen a live performance were enthralled by the WPA Theatre, and such a play as 'Let Freedom Ring', set in a bleak North Carolina mill town with stark stage sets, moved people profoundly. Neighbourhood groups in scores of cities established Little Theatres, staging plays in school auditoriums. Concerts by orchestras made up of volunteers and singing contests among locally organised choruses quickened community musical interests. Outdoor art shows held in public parks gave amateurs opportunity to exhibit their canvases. Public libraries were inundated with readers. All told, perhaps as important as WPA relief of immediate physical want was the city dweller's rediscovery that man does not live by bread alone.

Architecture received less direct encouragement but in many fields flowered none the less. Federal expenditures notwithstanding, public building in any one city, it is true, was limited first by the need of other communities for a share of PWA funds, and, second, by the precarious state of municipal budgets as long as the course of business recovery was uncertain. Fortunately, some public officials learned that economy and architectural beauty were not incompatible. The Junior High School designed by Richard Neutra for Los Angeles displayed a refreshing combination of strength, lightness, and harmony of line. When commercial building began to resume, private enterprise in New York built Rockefeller Center on Fifth Avenue, a complex of skyscrapers about a plaza with flower beds, sculpture, and a year-round sunken skating rink; less ambitious office buildings rose elsewhere in Manhattan and in other cities, but most of the work Frank Lloyd Wright scornfully placed in the category of 'slick architectural salesmanship'. Wright, his stature again recognised in the United States after a long eclipse, expressed his own concepts dramatically in an administration building he designed for the Johnson Wax Company at Racine, Wisconsin. But it was more largely in private residential building that Wright, Neutra, and William Lescaze, to name only three of the best-known innovators, exhibited their originality most fully—in the 'Falling Water' house, for example, that Wright built over a cascading stream, in the garden apartments and houses Neutra balanced on California hillsides, and in Lescaze's use of fenestration in a house on a narrow New York City lot.

The chief spur to the building industry, however, came from government subsidies for housing, and, in building liveable homes for the ill-housed third of the nation, a number of architects showed their versatility to best effect. Government funds financed the well-lighted Carl Mackley houses at Juniata Park in Philadelphia and William Lescaze's Williamsburg, an oasis in the Brooklyn slums which gave 1,600 families airy, sunlit quarters. John Holabird's Trumbull Park in Chicago was equally successful in supplying comfort and an inoffensive exterior in low-cost dwellings. In these and other cities-within-cities and in the garden apartments built in the suburbs by such organisations as the Metropolitan Life Insurance Company, the creators of Radburn could see their purposes fulfilled.

By no means all publicly subsidised housing measured up to those standards. Municipal financing of such projects was meagre before 1938. That year the total spent by local governments for commercial and residential building amounted to $3 million; by 1940 the figure had risen to $230 million. During the mid-1930s directors of slum clearance supported by federal or state funds aimed primarily at replacing filthy overcrowded tenements with sanitary accommodations for as many families as possible; aesthetics all too often dropped out of consideration. Hence again and again economy coupled with lack of imagination produced boxlike rows which left tenants feeling like occupants of loosely packed, aseptic sardine tins on grocery shelves.

When the federal Resettlement Administration, acting upon the principles of the defunct Regional Planning Association of America, undertook to encourage a dispersal of urban population by developing new towns suited to people of moderate means as well as the impoverished, Greenbelt, Maryland, materialised. Located within a half-hour's drive from mid-town Washington, the shops and houses surrounded by greensward and trees offered an attractive alternative to middle-class residential neighbourhoods in the city. Two other Greenbelt towns arose, but there the scheme ended. Pre-built, planned towns that seemed predicated upon organised community living had little appeal for Americans who could afford to choose.

Declining birth rates and, during the first half of the decade, outward migration from industrial centres did, however, check city growth. Among the nine largest cities, Philadelphia, Cleveland, St Louis, and Boston lost population between 1930 and 1940; Chicago added less than 1 per cent, New York 7·5. Many smaller communities barely held their own. Los Angeles, on the other hand, as financial centre of the expanding movie industry and its related enterprises, increased by 23 per cent, Detroit by 30·5 per cent, and Washington by 36·2 per cent. In the capital the rise in civil service employment from 73,000 posts to 129,800 accounted for much of the growth, but, of the 55,000 Negroes added to the population, at least 30,000 were in-migrants from the Deep South whose lack of education disqualified them for white collar jobs. Elsewhere, the extent of industrial recovery largely determined a city's fate, even where distribution of goods rather than manufacturing was the community's mainstay.

During 1933, while strikes spread across the country—involving grocery clerks in some places, shipyard hands in others, copper miners, and New York taxi drivers—federal officials and industrial executives sweated in Washington over codes which, under the terms of the National Industrial Recovery Act, every industry was to draft for itself. The codes proved hard to frame, harder still to make acceptable to government representatives intent on protecting the working man and the consumer, and hardest of all to enforce against companies who objected to some or all the provisions. Wage differentials between North and South made trouble for the cotton textile industry; the steel and automobile industries, where labour organisation had always been weak, balked at rules proposed for ending the open shop. Spokesmen for most industries protested at the imposition of minimum wages rates and ceiling on hours but no relaxation of the prohibition on price-fixing; eventually tacit re-interpretations of the anti-trust laws permitted industry considerable control over prices. The greatest stumbling block was the government's insistence on collective bargaining between management and labour, with labour represented by unions of its own choosing. Although some companies refused to sign such agreements, before the end of the year the NRA Blue Eagle was flying over factories in nearly every city. The foremost necessity was to start up production lines. Up to a point industrial management was eager to co-operate with the government. Everyone wanted labour peace. The details of how to ensure it would have to wait.

The rift came in carrying out the provision for union recognition —and workmen's, not company, unions. To workers that recognition was the key opening the door to every other advance. To many employers it represented loss of control over their own businesses, the death of free enterprise. Each side was convinced that it was fighting for its very life. In cities from coast to coast the battle lines formed in 1934.

The struggle in Minneapolis revolved around the truckers, for the city, the distributing centre for a wide region, depended more largely on her transport facilities than on her mills. The Citizens Alliance, an association of Minneapolis employers, in the past had held the line against unionism without much trouble. When a newly organised teamsters' local under politically radical leadership undertook to extract a contract from the Alliance in the spring of 1934, the employer group refused to deal with a body that seemed to doom every business in the city. The attempts of the Regional Labor Board to mediate were unavailing. In May the union leaders called a strike. For ten days it tied the city up 'as tight as a bull's eye in fly-time'. But the three-month nightmare had just begun. Negotiations for settlement stalled; the Alliance enlisted a 'citizen's army' to drive trucks and thus break the strike; other unions launched sympathetic strikes and, as both sides armed themselves with lead pipes and baseball bats, bloodshed followed. The state governor called out the National Guard; a truce, ended when the Alliance broke off the talks; police shootings of unarmed pickets; and then martial law. Here, one citizen said, was revolution; his son, a newspaperman, called the Alliance stand Fascism. In early August a few employers capitulated, and on the 21st suddenly the Alliance as a body agreed to the plan as modified by federal negotiators. Triumphant working people celebrated their victory in a twelve-hour demonstration.

San Francisco, unlike Minneapolis, had a long history of violence. The coming of NRA to the city and its official support of union recognition set off the fight at the waterfront which quickly turned into a general strike. Again the National Guard intervened, but the conflict spread up the coast to Seattle. Despite, or because of, Communist infiltration into the International Longshoreman's Union, the strike was bloodier but less well organised than the one in Minneapolis. The union head himself called it class warfare. It reached such proportions that several Cabinet members in Washington besought the President to send in federal forces. Ultimately, it angered without intimidating San Franciscans and collapsed with surprising abruptness. Once order had returned to the city, arbitration won the unions recognition and some of their specific demands. In Seattle and Oregon ports the struggle, if marked by less open violence, took the same general course. The shock of virtual civil war in major cities of the United States nevertheless remained.

Toledo, Ohio, faced a similar experience with a similar outcome for the electrical workers. But most of the union campaigns of 1934 netted labour nothing. During the month-long strike staged by the United Textile Workers in Providence, other Rhode Island cities, and in the South from North Carolina to Georgia, the street fighting between pickets and state troops sent in at mill owners' requests reached a deadliness that threatened to alienate any public sympathy for the mill hands' cause. In alarm the union called the strike off and acknowledged defeat. Nor did labour organisation on an industry-wide basis make any progress. Impotent company unions or small craft units were the rule in Detroit automobile plants, Pittsburgh's, Chicago's, and Birmingham's steel mills, and Akron's rubber tyre shops. There and in factories in other cities trouble simmered without producing effective action. The powerlessness of the President's mediation agency, the National Labor Relations Board, was self-evident.

Two developments changed the picture in 1935 and 1936, the first arising from congressional action, the second from the ranks of labour itself. Shortly after the Supreme Court declared the National Recovery Act unconstitutional a new act vested in the National Labor Relations Board power to enforce binding decisions in labour disputes. In 1936 at an AFL convention John L. Lewis of the United Mine Workers led a revolt that created the Congress of Industrial Organisations, a body that set about forming industrial unions which admitted unskilled labour along with skilled and might take Negro along with white. The United Automobile Workers was one of the first to demonstrate the potentialities of the CIO. Early in 1937 the UAW undertook a sit-down strike in the General Motors' plant in Flint, Michigan. The sit-down, whereby strikers occupied the factory and left to police, company detectives, and strike-breakers the problem of forcing a way in, was as effective as it was novel. In short order the General Motors' Corporation recognised the union and met most of its other demands. UAW sit-downs in Detroit against other companies were much longer drawn out. At the Ford plants in Dearborn hired private police ready to bludgeon and manhandle 'agitators' prevented labour organisers from so much as approaching the works. In and about Detroit during the late spring tension grew, finally released by a conference which the governor of Michigan arranged between John L. Lewis of the CIO and the Chrysler Company president. Again the UAW was victorious. Although Ford held out against unionisation for another four years, every other automobile company yielded. Within the union the acceptance of Negro members, if not invariably ungrudging, added to the sense of workers' solidarity. By 1940 Detroit had become a stronghold of organised labour, and industrial peace ruled.

Other cities saw much the same thing happen. Not all of them had to live through open warfare, and not all escaped periodic outbursts long after collective bargaining had become an accepted routine. In Southern cities any proposal to admit Negroes to union member-ship created a furore, and in many places reluctance to see the CIO supplant conservative AFL craft unions caused reactions. Jurisdic-tional squabbles among unions would in fact strain the mediating skills of the National Labor Relations Board for years to come. When business reverses, as in mid-1938, interrupted the slow up-ward climb towards stable employment and assured profits, indus-trial unrest again stirred, but the fear of full-scale bloody social revolution did not recur after 1938.

Doubtless the readiness of the urban middle classes to see some virtues in the labour movement was partly due to the press, not only the metropolitan dailies, but smaller newspapers carrying syndicated dispatches and home-made editorials, a press that fifteen years before had preached that the rich were above criticism from the hoi poloi, a press that had given as much space to chit-chat as to serious national and local problems. New Deal policymakers, for all their doctrinaire pronouncements, and the President, with touches of the messianic in his messages, gave city newspapers and journals a new point of view about what was news, and the press passed it on. If distinguished novels and volumes of poetry were fewer than in the 1920s, bookshops offered patrons such readable historical fiction as *Gone With the Wind* and greater quantities of thought-provoking fare than in the light-hearted decade, perhaps indeed enough to encourage John Dewey's hopes for the Great Community.

Meanwhile New Deal policies of using national resources to re-vive the economy and handle immediate social needs had unforeseen consequences for municipalities where old-style machine politicians had kept or recaptured some degree of control. In *The Last Hurrah*, a novel based on the career of James Curley, repeatedly mayor of Boston and one-time governor of Massachusetts, a hench-man accounts for his hero's final defeat. Who was responsible? 'F.D.R. Nobody else but.' For the welfare measures the President proposed and Congress enacted stripped the local boss of his patron-age, just as the repeal of the Prohibition amendment and the dis-appearance of bootlegging reduced the contributions he could expect from the underworld. If mayors of the calibre of Fiorello La Guardia of New York and Frank Murphy of Detroit were few, by the end of the 1930s scallawags like James Curley, with hearts 'as big as the state of Kansas', were equally few. While local adminis-trators in charge of the work relief, the pensions, and the housing loans that federal funds made possible were not invariably above reproach, most of them gave conscientious service. City police, freed of bootleggers, if not of gangsters, now were subject to lesser temptations and generally performed more efficiently. In Washing-ton they organised the Metropolitan Police Boys' Club so that potential juvenile delinquents could work off their energies and

G

frustrations in games and contests under rules laid down by them-selves with a minimum of police surveillance. After 1934 annual reports of a national City Manager's Association spread news of how members were coping with their problems. Although many of those problems were more acute than ever before in American history, citizens' discovery that solutions lay in their, not politicians', hands revived a sense of community, lost for a generation or more.

Some of that change probably sprang from a religious reawaken-ing. Rising church attendance testified to its strength. In Los Angeles, already home to various obscure religions such as Theosophy and New Thought, a peculiarly worldly variant of Christian Science, and in smaller California cities a dozen strange sects flourished along-side groups convinced that they had political and social panacea for hard times. More important, the century-old antagonism between Protestants and Catholics faded, and horror at Nazi persecutions of Jews reduced American anti-Semitism. Religious toleration also allowed white church-goers in big cities with large concentrations of Negroes to watch without alarm the appearance about 1938 of the Black Muslims, who believed that all evil originated with white men and that Allah would open Paradise only to Negroes who lived by Muslim precepts of asceticism and militance. Fortunately for white peace of mind, converts to that racist faith were few.

Despite the easing of economic pressures in urban communities after 1938, when the Nazi invasion of Poland set off World War II in September 1939, several million Americans were still on WPA or local relief rolls. White city people were better off than farmers—a fact emphasised by congressional preoccupation with farm bills—problems of urban unemployment, rehabilitation, slum clearance, public health, and education were still demanding close attention. Probably most of urban America was at least vaguely aware of the significance of Hitler's regime in Germany, but, except for the hand-ful of people who had been assisting Jewish scholars to escape and find teaching posts in American universities, few citizens regarded Europe's tragedy as a concern of the United States. America had troubles of her own. Yet within six months of the war's start, orders placed by the British and French purchasing commissions for aircraft, transport vehicles, and munitions were giving impetus to heavy industry in a score of cities, and the effects were seeping down into others. Within another seven months, Nazi victories on the continent and the Luftwaffe's intensive bombing of Britain had pushed the United States into full-scale industrial and military mobilisation for defence. Unemployment rapidly became a far lesser problem than training people to do the jobs that needed doing.

As the draft, under the new Selective Service Act, withdrew young men from civilian life, government agencies, industrial firms, and city school systems collaborated in opening vocational classes to train people as replacements in shops, factories, and offices. Simultaneously contracts to build barracks and furnish supplies to the military training camps benefited nearby communities. In the South, where most of the Army camps were located, quiet places, such as San Antonio, Texas, and Columbus, Georgia, buzzed with sudden activity. Month after month recruitment drives for skilled workmen gained momentum—for welders and mechanics to man the shipyards from Bremerton, Washington, and San Francisco to Bath, Maine, the aircraft shops in Seattle, Detroit, and Wichita, Michigan's automobile plants, and the tyre factories in Akron and Naugatuck, Connecticut. Steel mills, locomotive works, precision-tool and machine-tool shops, textile mills turning out uniform fabrics and blankets, shoe factories, and establishments endeavouring to convert to fire-arms manufacture—all needed hands. One consequence was a decision to train women as production line workers. In industrial cities across the country courses started before Pearl Harbor to instruct housewives, spinsters, and high-school girls in machine-shop techniques. When the United States found itself at war, shops where management and unions alike had for years raised an impenetrable barrier against females accepted them unenthusiastically but without protest. At the same time the ever-growing mountain of paperwork involved in increasing the output of goods tenfold put a premium also on typing and clerical skills.

Negro opportunities, however, did not widen as fully as coloured people expected. In Northern cities as well as Southern, companies repeatedly chose to avoid the complications of hiring coloured hands. Even where Negroes were union members, racial discrimination tended to militate against promotion, irrespective of their skills. And unhappily hurried training on top of meagre school education often limited those skills. Whether or not prejudice always controlled hiring and promotion policies, Negroes felt sure it generally did. They had had scant experience in organised protest. During the depths of the depression a group in Washington had successfully used the boycott as a weapon to open up some three hundred jobs to Negroes in white-owned stores located in coloured neighbourhoods. Memory of that modest victory inspired leaders in the spring of 1941 to enlist some 50,000 coloured men in a July 4 march on Washington to present their demands for fair treatment to Congress and the President. When the attempts of the temperate Mayor La Guardia of New York and flustered government officials failed to dissuade them, on June 25 the White House acted: an Executive Order on Fair Employment Practices instructed every company under contract with the United States and every federal agency to eliminate racial discrimination; proven violation of the order would result in contract cancellation. Negroes called off the march.

The long-term effects were at once less and more than anticipated. Evasions of the order were not uncommon. The migration of coloured workers to West Coast industrial establishments offended Los Angelenos. Growlings echoed around the one-time earthly paradise now dotted with black colonies. In Detroit a race riot broke out in 1943 fanned by the resentment of Southern whites at having to work side by side with 'nigras' in the automobile and aircraft shops. Later investigation by the FBI and military authorities in and about the plants proved that native fascist agitators had instigated the fight that began on a bridge to the Belle Isle amusement park, but Detroiters in many walks of life were caught up in the violence before hysteria subsided. In Connecticut towns when the manpower shortage forced machine shops to import Negro workmen, nobody would provide the newcomers with living quarters; they had to come and go by truck daily fifty miles each way. The mass movement of Negro families cityward created

teeming ghettoes again and again; the President's anti-discrimina-
tion order did not extend to housing. And a new aggressiveness
among coloured men who knew they now had legal rights during
working hours heightened tensions in many cities. Yet the eventual
consensus ran that Negroes had won a more secure place for themselves than the American urban world had ever before allowed
them.

City dwellers of every breed had discomforts to endure. Some
600,000 temporary and 200,000 permanent housing units built with
government money provided accommodations for industrial workers and service men's families before the war was over, but until 1944
serious overcrowding was general in and about industrial centres.
Privately financed residential building fell to a quarter of the 1940
total. At Willow Run outside Detroit where the great aircraft works
of the Ford Motor Company packed some 30,000 men into a small
space, wage earners who were taking home perhaps as much as $200
a week had to live for months under conditions little better than
those of slum families before the war. Architectural charm was no
consideration; a Nissen hut would do. Trailer parks, a new
phenomenon, eased the congestion in some communities, but sanitary facilities were often sketchy, and the temporary character of
the trailer camps encouraged carelessness among inmates. Price
controls administered in Washington and regional offices from
January 1942 onwards kept commodities and rents at fixed dollar
levels but could not enlarge the supply of goods or space. Tyre and
gasoline rationing limited the distance at which anyone wanted to
live from his job. Public transport was slow and wretchedly un-
comfortable during rush hours, and, as most plants ran three shifts,
trolleys and buses had to operate twenty-four hours a day.

Probably the forty-eight-hour week, or on some jobs a sixty-
hour week, was the single most disruptive factor in family life.
Able-bodied fathers and mothers with demanding war jobs had
little time at home; standing in line to market cut into that time
further. So some children were left to their own devices after school
hours, some to the care of elderly relatives, some to the supervision
of volunteers at play centres and nurseries. If welfare experts foresaw
troubled parent-child relationships in the post-war world, the

temptation of two weekly or bi-weekly pay cheques to a family, combined with a patriotic urge to 'carry on', usually over-rode objections.

Those circumstances, together with mounting school enrolments, placed added responsibilities upon school teachers. Enrolments, particularly in city high schools, had expanded enormously during the 1930s for obvious reasons. Boys and girls over fourteen years of age had been unable to get jobs, after 1937 a good many states had lengthened the number of years of obligatory schooling, and about the same time most city school systems had multiplied business and vocational courses and changed the educational approach in the lower grades to 'child-oriented' curricula in order to heighten pupil interest. But recruitment of teachers had rarely been commensurate with growing school populations, and, as the more elaborate methods of instruction had frequently required summer study for teachers and extra hours during the school year, staffs were badly overburdened before the war came. Under war conditions over-worked teachers seldom felt they were meeting the challenge adequately, especially as they were often expected to serve on draft boards and undertake similar extraneous public duties. In 'impacted areas' near camps and government installations federal subsidies for schools sometimes enabled cities to offer excellent schooling, but more often school systems laboured under handicaps reminiscent of World War I. Few municipalities saw fit to put more than minimal sums into maintaining the physical equipment of their schools.

Although municipal spending for public health rose nearly 16 per cent between 1940 and 1944, cities spent on an average 5 per cent less on policing and 18 per cent less on relief and welfare services, partly because the federal government and American Red Cross chapters carried the burden of helping servicemen's families. Un-employment compensation in 1944 dropped to less than a seventh the figure for 1940. Logically enough perhaps, communities post-poned capital investments in building and highway projects. Sharply increased federal income-tax rates, on the other hand, skilful cam-paigns for subscriptions to government savings' bonds, and fund drives for good works ranging from Community War Chests to China Relief added to citizens' financial obligations. People everywhere gave generously but complained loudly and lived for the day when the war would be over, the 'boys' would return, and peace would permit life to resume its ordinary course. Cities could then get on with the interrupted jobs of slum clearance and road building, expanding recreation facilities, improving schools, and fostering the arts.

8

THE POPULATION EXPLOSION AND

A CHANGING URBAN WORLD

Any expectation that American city life would resume in the post-World War II era where it had left off in 1940 quickly proved illusory. Some of the old bones of contention had worn thin. Protestant-Catholic feuding faded into insignificance, virtually erased by the autumn of 1960 with the election of the first Roman Catholic President. In the economic realm, some issues took new form. The main problems were the unforeseen and those that acquired such intensity as to seem unfamiliar: the overwhelming growth of city and metropolitan regional populations that threatened in some sections of the country to leave no open country whatsoever, the rising number of school children to be educated and, at the other end of the age spectrum, the multiplying over age-65 groups; the devastating inroads of automobile traffic which increasingly transformed residential neighbourhoods of central cities into noisy, smog-laden passageways; and a mounting racial consciousness focussed upon Negro civil rights and schooling. Most of these situation were closely intertwined. Search for solutions failed to open up sure paths through the tangle. Only one fact was clear by 1960: all American social history had become in essence urban history.

In the immediate post-war years, with the expiration of the

labour-management truce observed in industry for the duration, strikes again broke out, with labour demands frequently aimed at fringe benefits like paid vacations, as well as higher wages and escalator clauses adjusting rates to living costs. At the same time contests between unions were not infrequent. At the Boeing plant in Seattle the long-established machinists' local felt itself betrayed by the teamsters who made a deal with the company management and, after driving strike-breakers through the picket lines for five months, won jurisdiction over the aircraft mechanics. But by the late 1940s the governmental mediation machinery, despite occasional creakings, generally operated well enough to settle disputes fairly quickly, and to leave industrial communities without fear of again seeing class warfare like that of the 1930s.

Increasing automation, to be sure, brought unemployment in its wake. In 1950 the compensation states were paying out to jobless people ran to $1,849 million, over three and a half times the figure for 1940. Where 200 hands had run the looms in a Holyoke, Massachusetts, mill in the 1930s, fifteen years later the great weave shed contained two people watching the automatic machines turn out the fine fabrics. Chemists and optical experts, not lens grinders, held the reponsible jobs at the glass works in Corning, New York, where the huge 200-inch plastic lens for the Palomar observatory was receiving its final touches in 1950. The International Business Machines plant in Hartford, Connecticut, became a laboratory manned chiefly by Ph.D.s, and, as the computors and duplicating equipment coming from the works replaced hand-operated adding machines and ordinary typewriters in offices throughout the country, jobs in Hartford's typewriter factories shrank. Direct long-distance dialling reduced the number of telephone operators over the country to a few hundred. In the construction industry, men driving bulldozers and controlling intricate cranes supplanted the crews of diggers who in the past had excavated cellar holes. Inventions and novel methods of producing goods did of course create new jobs, but the steady trend of industry towards reliance on engineers and men with scientific background left old-time machine operators with thinning prospects. Intensive retraining might reinstate some of the younger men, but technological unemployment remained a disturbing element in the economic picture. To the worsening plight of manual workers the declining ratio of blue-collar to white-collar jobs bore witness: in Philadelphia, for 150 years predominantly a manufacturing city, 40 per cent of all jobs in 1960 were white-collar, and in Houston, centre of a burgeoning oil industry and of new electronics enterprises, 47 per cent were white-collar.

Service jobs took up much of the slack. Garage mechanics, TV and radio repairmen, barbers and beauty shop operators, people in charge of cleaning and self-service laundromat establishments, and thousands of others made out well enough as long as they stayed on the payroll. But once a person over forty-five or at most fifty lost his job, blue-collar, white-collar, or some of both, he was likely to have a hard time getting another. While actuarial tables showed that he might well live another twenty-five years, as a bread-winner he was generally done for, unless he had unusual capacities. In the nuclear age to start at the bottom at the age of fifty to qualify for a new occupation meant competing with men in their early twenties fresh from special schooling. Even government agencies which ordinarily gave special consideration to the physically handicapped were loath to engage the 'elderly'. Wedded to the youth cult as Americans were, younger people were slow to comprehend that here was a problem that concerned them as well as the old: people with jobs would have to support most of those without.

The backlog of housing needs that had accumulated during the war, however, kept the building trades busy for a decade and more after V-J Day. Public and privately financed developments mush-roomed within city limits and still more profusely in the nearby countryside. Concentric rings of housing sprang up beyond the older suburbs of central cities, much of it monotonous in layout and shoddy in construction but almost immediately sold and occupied. Suburban sprawl, before 1950 rarely taken very seriously, suddenly became a source of anxiety to both city and suburban administrators. By the mid-1950s the uneasy prophecy that before 1975 the five hundred miles from above Boston southward to Washington and beyond would be on unbroken built-up stretch, a 'megalopolis', looked perilously accurate. Another solid band of cities and suburbs was likely to reach from Buffalo to Detroit and on to Chicago; estimates ran that seven or eight more 200-mile-long expanses of continuous city would appear in the rest of the United States. Southern California already constituted a virtual megalopolis; there only dwindling water resources provided a semblance of check on population density. In all metropolitan complexes the need of regional rather than municipal controls became increasingly evident, whether to regulate water consumption and sewage disposal, or to salvage open spaces for parks, lay out throughways, and apportion costs fairly. Despite joint commissions to deal with some of these matters for Greater New York, Greater Boston, Greater Washington, and several other metropolitan areas, political boundaries handicapped intelligent planning and execution.

From 1946 onwards, a growing army of professional planners set about drafting schemes for the orderly renewal of central cities. The task usually involved the re-location of families displaced by the demolition of old dwellings, devising a balance between expensive and inexpensive housing in restored areas, widening of highways and construction of new, and, in some cases, clearing away every building in order to provide open spaces within the heart of the city. Pittsburghers fixed their attention on redeeming the oldest part of the business district at the junction of the Monongahela and Allegheny rivers where the Ohio begins its turbulent westward flow. Sand blasting the smoke of decades from old structures, removing others, erecting new, ripping out the tracks of railroad sidings, and planting grass and trees at the tip of the land produced the 'Golden Triangle', acclaimed as a dramatic example of how united community action could transform ugliness into beauty; if a certain sterility diminished that beauty, it was nevertheless clean and uncluttered. San Francisco's efforts went chiefly into super-highway construction which threaded the city from the Golden Gate to the Bay Bridge with elevated automobile roads. Embattled citizens in scores of communities struggled against strangling 'spaghetti', the name anguished architects assigned to the throughways and loops of feeders which highway engineers deemed essential.

Meanwhile most of the densely populated older cities directed renewal at slum clearance and new housing projects. In Washington, one of the first cities to undertake a large-scale physical rehabilitation programme, bulldozers razed all but a half-dozen buildings in the entire section south-west of the Capitol. The character of the rebuilding evoked protests over what some citizens considered a disproportionate number of high-priced town houses and luxury apartments, but other people were enthusiastic; at least the rat-infested alley dwellings were gone. On Chicago's south side some three square miles adjoining the University of Chicago campus were subjected to similar, albeit less all-inclusive, demolition and to renewal which met with a similar compound of criticism and commendation. Wherever cities sought to combine new low-cost housing with the development of neighbourhoods containing also upper-class residents, special difficulties cropped up. Sometimes the architectural effects were pleasing, sometimes the reverse. Always the rising cost of land imposed restrictions on architectural design.

The sheer mass of people to house heightened difficulties. The country over, as the birth rate rose, the death rate dropped. Accompanying the early marriages of the war and first post-war years was a reversion to the nineteenth-century pattern of having large families. From the 62 per cent of males over fourteen years of age in 1940 who were married, the percentage climbed to 71 per cent in two decades. Although the birth rate then levelled off, the lengthened life of adults pushed population totals upwards. Not every city grew. Between 1950 and 1960 Philadelphia lost 3·3 per cent of her inhabitants, Detroit nearly 9, and Washington 36·8 per cent, largely to her suburbs. Los Angeles, on the contrary, increased by almost 26 per cent, Houston by 57, and smaller places on an average of 3·5 per cent. But even cities with slightly declining populations had to halt decay by some rebuilding.

Unhappily the belief of the 1930s and 1940s that better housing would make better neighbourhoods and so better citizens proved fallacious again and again in the 1950s, unless what housing authorities had deemed better were in fact worse. The clusters of ten to a dozen twelve- to sixteen-storey apartment buildings that replaced solid blocks of squalid tenements in New York's Bronx, for example, quickly turned into high-rise slums. The open space about them had no beneficial effects on the life within the warrens in which the very elevators served as barriers between family and family. The chief difference between the old slums and the new, one newspaperman reported, was that parents who formerly could maintain a semblance of discipline by yelling out of the window at Tony or Johnny in the street below now lost all knowledge of how their children spent their time once the apartment doors closed behind them, and so all parental control evaporated. In those great impersonal, dehumanised hives rising skywards in New York, Chicago, Boston, and other big cities, family life, so far from acquiring new dignity, simply disintegrated. Nor did family ties endure elsewhere. The character of city living quarters appeared to have little bearing upon the character of their occupants' behaviour.

While juvenile delinquency had long been a familiar affliction of American cities, and especially during the depression, the dimensions it assumed in the late 1940s and the 1950s baffled police departments, school administrators, and conscientious parents. If the number of mothers who had taken full-time war jobs accounted initially for much of the wholesale rebellion against authority, ten years later the explanation seemed too simple and certainly did not cover the cases among young people of the so-called 'better families'. The gangs of juveniles warring against each other in city slums were frighteningly intractable; when they carried out knifings, garrotings, and hold-ups against adults as well, they terrorised entire neighbourhoods. But in relatively well-to-do suburban communities, in turn, vandal-ism, car thefts, and forms of violence, sometimes attributed to a widening use of narcotics among high-school students, challenged the rule of law. Small wonder that the sums local governments spent on police protection rose from $434 million in 1946 to $691 million in 1950 and to $1,290 million in 1957. Youth counsellors attached to police, welfare, and school departments offered one approach to the gangs; another lay in organised recreation directed by church groups, Rotary, Kiwanis, and Lions' Clubs, and fraternal orders such as the Catholic Knights of Columbus. Yet doubts at times assailed the most earnest citizen as to whether those measures were at best more than palliatives.

Whether the rootlessness of thousands of middle- and upper-class families contributed to the social instability seen in all American cities was another question. Certainly the frequent geographic moves of men in white-collar occupations lent an impermanence to the civic leadership upon which communities could draw. To cite an extreme example, Houston, Texas, repeatedly saw energetic newcomers purchase houses, settle in, and within three months depart, because the policy of companies with a dozen branches usually dictated periodic transfers of minor executives. Scientists moved from laboratories in Pasadena and Berkeley to research centres in Bloomington, Oak Ridge, or Washington, while others reversed the route. If doctors, lawyers, and public school teachers were generally fixed in a given spot, members of other professions tended to shift from place to place far more frequently than before World War II. Nascent community feeling suffered from the constricted growing time.

One conviction was universal. Whether long-time resident or citizen on the wing, the city dweller believed improved schooling and more of it a must. Without some training in science how could the younger generation fit into jobs that called for an understanding of cybernetics? And as electronic brains disposed in minutes of tasks that used to take human grey matter days and weeks, must not children and adults learn new uses for leisure? While new school houses went up, school superintendents experimented with new curricula and the use of visual aids to learning, such as television. Realisation, moreover, that textbooks written for children who grew up in a semi-rural middle-class setting were inappropriate for city children who had never seen a cow or an unfrozen chicken led to a re-examination of the basic tools of elementary education. When the first Soviet Sputnik shattered American complacency about American technological superiority, courses in mathematics and science received new emphasis. The Library of Congress immediately lengthened the hours during which the reading rooms would be open to the public. Still not all children could become physicists or engineers or even experts in the humanities, and since leisure, wanted or unwanted, promised to become an everyday commodity, educators gave thought to training the younger generation to occupations that would have seemed like trimmings in the

Progressive era. Some high schools and teachers' colleges added courses in music appreciation, art history, story telling, playground direction, more rarely the dance, household repairs, and 'home-making', meaning everything from setting a dinner table properly and sending children to bed promptly to arranging flowers. If much of this instruction had appeal chiefly to females, the rising proportion of women in the United States partly justified the selection.

In the interim, the $45·8 million that cities spent on public education in 1946 rose to $76·8 million, and 970,000 new school employees swelled the two million of 1946, but the dizzy pace at which pupil enrolments increased tended to outrun school resources. By the early 1960s every Monday morning a Chicago school administrator had to find space for a hundred additional Negro pupils just arrived from Mississippi, and a Los Angeleno asserted that the California city needed a hundred new schools every month. Furthermore, inasmuch as virtually every citizen above the rank of day labourer felt his children must have a college education, junior colleges multiplied, many of them supported by city taxes, and state and municipal universities where 5,000 undergraduates had been a pre-war norm enrolled 15–30,000.

At the college level much of the increase was undoubtedly a long-lasting consequence of the federal legislation of 1944 known as the 'G.I. Bill of Rights', a law whereby every person who had spent at least a few months in the Armed Services was entitled upon an honourable discharge to some schooling at government expense. Depending upon his length of service, he might take anywhere from a semester to three years of special courses, college undergraduate work, or graduate study without paying tuition; the intent of the law was to ensure his losing no educational opportunity because of serving his country. Occasionally the Veterans Administration protested at a man's using his 'G.I. rights' to take, say, dancing lessons, but most of the three million and more veterans who took advantage of their privileges chose to pursue academic subjects. The demand for college teachers rose proportionately after 1946 and, when G.I. rights expired in the mid-1950s, was sustained by the flood of 'war babies', who by then were approaching an age to enter college.

Steady progress towards giving every American child, white or coloured, extensive and thorough education unhappily suffered a setback in the late 1950s, for a Supreme Court decision of May 1954 declaring racial segregation in public schools unconstitutional set a match to a slow-burning fuse. School boards in border cities from the District of Columbia to Kentucky set about complying with instructions to integrate schools with 'all deliberate speed', but segregationists in the Deep South ignored the ruling. With state endorsement, a number of Southern cities that had attempted to forestall the court decision by endeavouring to make their coloured schools as good as their white adopted a scheme of granting subsidies to white private schools in fashion that would perpetuate a dual system: tax-supported schools for coloured children, tax-subsidised for white. Open rebellion flared out in Little Rock, capital of Arkansas, in 1957 when the first handful of Negro children crossed the portals of a theretofore white public high school. An air-borne unit of the United States Army eventually restored order of sorts, while the state governor breathed defiance, bullies threatened moderates, and the superintendent of schools together with a lone newspaper editor stood courageously by their moral guns. The superintendent was dismissed but, like the editor, found himself a hero in the eyes of many Americans. Yet despite the turmoil, integration in the Little Rock schools survived, its initial token character gradually widening in scope. And one by one, other Southern cities followed her example.

The Arkansas battle meanwhile gave the signal that widened the contest to include all forms of civil rights. By 1959 coloured people were beginning to defy southern Jim Crow laws and custom by occupying front seats on city and inter-city buses. Within a year or two, Negroes joined by a few white sympathisers conducted 'sit-ins' at racially segregated restaurants, organised non-violent picketing, and went to jail as disturbers of the peace. In the South the struggle focussed above all upon Negro voter registration, for in communities where Negroes outnumbered whites, as was the case in much of Mississippi, political equality might inexorably put an end to white social and economic supremacy. In the North the conflict centred on 'open housing', meaning the legal right of a coloured person to own or occupy quarters wherever he could afford to live whether in a substantial city neighbourhood or in an exclusive suburb of affluent whites. While Negro militance mounted and pressures rose for a strong federal civil rights act, temperate citizens of every complexion acknowledged the difficulty of changing century-old social attitudes.

Yet the very awareness of discrimination and injustice in a dozen areas of American life in itself marked a change. In the past, an American historian noted recently, 'so few people cared about civil liberties that the score on undemocratic practices was scarcely kept at all'. At the end of the 1950s men were keeping the score. Granting that the protection of civil liberties was primarily a matter for the courts, whereas observation of civil rights must depend more largely upon the readiness of private persons to recognise them, the score keepers began to tally both. The fact pointed to a newly sensitised social conscience. Money from philanthropic foundations poured into studies of how to proceed constructively, and thousands of earnest men and women dedicated most of their waking hours to trying to right old wrongs without creating needless new restrictions of individual liberty.

Christian ministers and Jewish rabbis frequently took the lead in these campaigns. A growing movement among Protestant denominations to form union churches perhaps strengthened their hands. Accompanying the spread of a Social Gospel now directed primarily at race relations instead of labour-versus-capital controversies was a religious revivalism faintly reminiscent of the Great Awakening of the eighteenth century. Evangelists preaching against personal sin drew huge crowds; from San Diego to New York, Billy Graham held audiences of 50,000 spellbound week after week. Radio and television studios gave Sunday morning programmes over exclusively to the sermons of popular pastors. If the result was at times a form of self-righteousness only dimly linked to the Golden Rule, the influence churchmen exercised in the United States of 1960 was nevertheless a phenomenon unpredictable twenty years before.

Social routines also changed, irrespective of concepts of justice or religion. As domestic servants, since 1942 a vanished species, failed to reappear, families in the middle- and upper-income brackets had to make do with labour-saving household equipment and an occasional cleaning woman paid by the hour. Partly out of necessity, partly as a hobby, 'do it yourself' came to be the rule. Frozen foods purchased at self-service markets in neighbourhood shopping centres took the place of elaborate dishes on family dinner tables. Young parents formed 'baby-sitting pools', and teen-agers picked up pocket money by evening 'sitting'. TV sets, a status symbol in 1950, became a matter of course by 1960 in the humblest household. In both city and suburb, social differences were chiefly visible to the naked eye in the expensiveness of the family car; the two-car family naturally outranked the one-car. Cassandras saw in this spread of uniform modes of behaviour the last steps towards the 'dead level of harassed mediocrity' which Josiah Royce had dreaded fifty years before. But the levelling process seemed to more optimistic observers to justify itself by raising the standards of the people upon whom a genuine democracy must depend.

Critics of this mass civilisation tended to give little weight to the enlarging role of the creative arts. Certainly a good many of the 20,000 books published yearly in American cities lacked high literary quality, and *How to Make Friends and Influence People* sold more widely than Ann Lindbergh's poems or John Steinbeck's novels. The miles of glass- and aluminium-banded walls hemming in the canyons of city business districts were frequently more overpowering than beautiful; the exquisite proportions of an occasional public building afforded only meagre relief. The sculpture emplaced in public parks was often so wanting in originality that a member of the National Capital Fine Arts Commission, dismayed at the furore aroused by the design proposed for a memorial to Franklin D. Roosevelt, implied that American taste in 1960 was as childish as it was when every town in the country was erecting a stone effigy to the Civil War dead. Picture galleries contained larger quantities of native American canvases, but who, asked the disgruntled, perceived the difference between the good and the bad? Did it matter that amateur photography had become a nearly universal hobby, or that some movie films were works of art, or that Little Theatre groups had sprung up in small cities as well as big, as long as television programmes nightly presented the most vulgar and unwholesome kind of show to an acquiescent public? The four or five ballet companies in the United States performed for relatively small audiences, and the vogue for square dancing was limited. If newsboys listened to transistor radios while they delivered papers and high-school students and adults played in neighbourhood orchestras, could anyone who heard the recordings of popular disc jockeys believe that music meant anything but noise to urban America?

The mere enumeration of these varied potential interests nevertheless suggested a rising preoccupation with elements of life that most of nineteenth-century America had considered non-essential. In each realm, discriminating taste was developing concurrently with popular acceptance of the second rate, and, hopeful social planners argued, the spread of leisure would gradually lead untutored people to a sharper perception of beauty.

The United States was not alone in confronting new social forces of frightening magnitude. But to a good many people the discovery came as a shock that American wisdom was not infallible, that *It Can't Happen Here* might be more than a tale with which to scare innocents. Here, as in the United Kingdom, rural poverty and rural education were coming under urban influences, but American education had not kept pace with the diffusion of political power, even though voting rights, wider spread in the eighteenth-century nation than anywhere else on earth, still failed to include coloured citizens in some of the states. Political leadership once exercised by the rich and well-born in the growing cities of the New World had passed into other hands, while the possession of riches had broadened. The term 'well-born' itself was no longer clearly defined. Regrets for a simpler, rural past, with its detachment from the troubles of the rest of the world would not turn back the clock. Jet plane travel, intercontinental telephone lines, and space-platform communication relays now brought the upheavals of Africa's interior to the very doorstep of the resident of Oshkosh, Wisconsin, St. Augustine, Florida, and Bellingham, Washington. A complex urban society now reluctantly recognised itself as part of a global civilisation.

The life-giving core of an agricultural nation for well over a century, the American city had long possessed an organic quality intimately associated with place. By the 1960s natural setting mattered less than size in differentiating one city from another.

Business, cultural interests, and social problems of the biggest cities, irrespective of location, were more nearly alike than were those of a metropolis and her regional satellites. And the larger the city the more surely the massed weight of reinforced concrete and stone, structural steel and glass, dehumanised wide areas within her limits. Except for a few storeys in the height of office buildings, New York's financial district looked much like Los Angeles's or Chicago's or Detroit's or Houston's; if the slums of one varied externally from those of the others, the inner conflicts in all were virtually identical. Among smaller, like-sized cities similarities were only less pronounced. While the ease and rapidity of communication accounted for much of this ironing out of the distinctiveness of individual cities, the more affluent half of American society probably contributed to it by constantly shifting from locality to locality.

At the same time in cities the country over, needs outran local resources. Even wealthy residential communities rarely commanded sufficient tax income to handle all their civic affairs without state or federal assistance. State governments depended upon federal funds for help in meeting city unemployment and rehabilitation payments, highway programmes, housing and urban renewal projects, and such wants as sewage disposal and an enlarged water supply which affected several cities of a region. The problems of urban America, in short, had become a national problem. Yet the political philosophy of the United States still relegated them to the category of local questions. The creation of a federal Department of Urban Affairs comparable to the Department of Agriculture, a proposal first tendered early in the century in Theodore Roosevelt's day, received little serious attention. Whereas the 1962 budget for the Department of Agriculture ran to some $7·4 billion, the sum allotted to urban problems totalled about $400 million, much of it 'authorised' but not appropriated. Agricultural research and farm subsidies yearly produced crop surpluses, and, although big corporate proprietors rather than small independent farmers reaped most of the benefits, consumers throughout the country gained from the abundant food supply. The American people recognised the well-being of the farm as a national concern. They were not yet seeing the city in a similar light.

Lavish spending in itself could supply few satisfactory answers to urban difficulties. For example, the vast national highway system, intended to bind the country together, worsened traffic congestion within many cities and, in avoiding routes through business districts, cut through residential neighbourhoods, making them isolated islands washed by exhaust fumes and subjected to the roar and dangers of fast-moving vehicles. The Federal Housing Administration, it is true, and the much newer Community Facilities Administration, set up in the mid-1950s to assist states and cities in planning and financing essential improvements, dispensed expert advice along with federal money, but neither agency worked on any comprehensive national plan; officials in one regional branch seldom had more than a vague idea of what was afoot in another. While it was common knowledge that the crime and human misery in Harlem and the ghettoes of other big cities had not diminished with new apartment building and more extensive policing, discussion of better possible remedies won a limited hearing in the nation at large.

Arguing that the persistence of cities' most acute social ills was largely due to the rigidity of the physical environment and that half-measures could not change it, students of the city jungles were beginning to insist that only a wholesale transplanting of thousands of their inhabitants to new towns in new surroundings could restore degraded slum dwellers to the ranks of responsible human beings, and only then could city life recapture its lost dignity. The doubting Thomas pointed out that this line of argument ignored New Deal experience in vainly attempting resettlement of city dwellers and, more important, by-passed the basic problem of the population explosion. To 'new town' advocates neither objection seemed valid. In the 1930s, they explained, plans for population redistribution had been robbed of urgency by the declining birth rate. Furthermore, since 1940 the United States had devised much more efficient methods of financing home building and the acquisition of large tracts of land. New construction techniques now could reduce costs, especially on big undertakings, whether executed by a partnership of public and private enterprise or, as in the case of the Tennessee Valley Authority, by the government alone. Granted that continuing unchecked population growth at the lowest level of society might rapidly turn new towns into new slums, could anyone envisage teaching people ridden by anger and despair to resort voluntarily to birth control, even were the price of the newly developed contraceptive pill to drop? Planned parenthood could only take effect in an environment of hopefulness where families had some reason to think of the future.

Maladjustments in the economy and several million unemployed notwithstanding, in the early 1960s a larger proportion of people in the United States were living in comfort and security than in any country at any period in history. The very extent of that comfort heightened the difficulties of persuading its beneficiaries that drastic action might be necessary to preserve it. Certainly they were unlikely to sanction a scheme of sterilising the irresponsibles and the depraved at the bottom, or indeed higher levels, of the social pyramid. Whether public opinion would endorse the new town proposal, or support a large, thoroughly trained, domestic Peace Corps working in the cities, or demand a totally novel approach or none at all was still a matter of doubt. In American urban life change was the only certainty.

SELECT BIBLIOGRAPHY

BRIDENBAUGH, Carl, *Cities in the Wilderness*. New York, 1955
Cities in Revolt. New York, 1955

BUREAU OF THE CENSUS, *Historical Statistics of the United States Colonial Times to 1957*, Washington, D.C., 1960

GLAAB, Charles N. (ed.), *The American City, A Documentary History*. Homewood, Ill., 1963

GREEN, Constance McLaughlin, *American Cities in the Growth of the Nation*. London, 1957

HAYS, Samuel P., *The Response to Industrialism, 1885–1914*. Chicago, 1957

LARKIN, Oliver W., *Art and Life in America*, rev. ed. New York, 1960

LEUCHTENBURG, William E., *The Perils of Prosperity*. Chicago, 1957

LUBOVE, Roy, *Community Planning in the 1920s*. Pittsburgh, 1963

MCKELVEY, Blake, *The Urbanization of America*. New Brunswick, New Jersey, 1963

PAULIN, C. O., *Atlas of the Historical Geography of the United States*. Washington, 1932

SCHLESINGER, Arthur M., *The Rise of the City, 1878–1898*. New York, 1933

SCHLESINGER, Arthur M., Jr., *The Coming of the New Deal*. Boston, 1959

WHITE, MORTON and LUCIA, *The Intellectual versus the City*. Cambridge, 1962

WILLIAMSON, Harold F. (ed.), *The Growth of the American Economy*, 2nd ed. New York, 1951

INDEX

184 Index